ATHENIAN DEMOCRACY

ATHENIAN DEMOCRACY:

Triumph or Travesty?

Edited by JILL N. CLASTER

New York University

HOLT, RINEHART AND WINSTON

New York • Chicago • San Francisco • Toronto • London

Cover illustration: The Porch of
the Caryatids, Erechtheum, Athens.
(Greek National Tourist Office)

CONTENTS

INTRODUCTION

"Were there such a thing as a nation of Gods, it would be a democracy. So perfect a form of government is not suited to mere men." The words are Rousseau's, and they suggest part of the difficulty of interpreting, objectively, the failure of Athenian democracy.

Though democratic institutions existed elsewhere in Greece, the credit for developing the first fully mature democracy belongs to Athens; in this she was the school, not only of Hellas, but of modern Europe as well. The great age of Athens' democracy was the fifth century; before the end of the fourth century it had been obliterated. From its inception the democracy invoked heated argument among Greece's foremost thinkers and the debate has not grown stale. The problems that modern historians seek to resolve are as relevant now as they were in classical Greece: What fosters and what hinders democracy? Was the government of Athens, even at its height, a triumph or a travesty of the democratic ideal?

In these readings the major issue is Athenian democracy, its character and its collapse. But the word "democracy," even as it applies to this first experiment in democratic government, is weighed down with judgments about its value as a political system. Many historians bring to their study of this problem the conviction that democracy must be, as Rousseau suggested, the perfect form of government. They find the basis for their faith in the text of Pericles' moving panegyric to Athens, recorded by Thucydides as the *Funeral Oration*. Although their conviction gives this problem a particular pertinence for the twentieth century, it often leads to idealizing the practices of Athenian democracy, or to forgiving the system its trespasses.

Those historians, on the other hand, who are critical of democracy have tended to see the Athenian failure as necessary and inevitable, brought about by weaknesses inherent in the form or spirit of the rule of the people. This point of view is part of a tradition that reaches back to the classical world, where the antidemocratic literature far outweighed the literature that supported democracy. Plato did not open the assault, but his pessimism about the ability of democracy to solve its problems has influenced a good deal of subsequent scholarship on Athenian government.

1

Finally, there are the disillusioned, the historians who expect too much of the Greeks and therefore judge them too harshly. In the essay which introduces the readings, Herbert J. Muller warns us that because the Greeks invented the ideal of freedom (and with it, democracy) is not sufficient reason to expect that they necessarily lived up to it. In this view there were limitations on the classical ideal as well as limitations on the Greeks themselves. The failure, then, has sometimes appeared as a betrayal, and we might do well to keep in mind what Carl Becker wrote when, assessing the reality as against the ideal of our modern democracy, he said that "life and history have an inveterate habit of betraying the ideal aspirations of men. . . . But while a little betrayal is a normal thing, too much is something that calls for explanation."[1]

The main institutions through which the people ruled Athens were the *ecclesia* (the popular Assembly), the *heliaea* (the popular courts), which were given increased importance by Cleisthenes at the close of the sixth century, and the Council of Five Hundred, which he established. It was particularly in the first two that the sovereignty of the people was most fully vested. The last conservative bars to participation in the Assembly and the courts were removed by Pericles in the middle of the fifth century. However familiar, his *Funeral Oration* is still the best single statement of the claims the full democracy made for itself. Here is what Pericles said: "[Our constitution] favors the many instead of the few; this is why it is called a democracy. If we look to the laws, they afford equal justice to all in their private differences; if to social standing, advancement in public life falls to reputation for capacity, class considerations not being allowed to interfere with merit. . . . The freedom which we enjoy in government extends also to our ordinary life."[2] Majority rule, equality before the law, personal freedom—these were the basic assumptions of Athenian democracy.

Although the Athenians bequeathed us their conception of equality and freedom—and they were themselves "confessors of the name"—the problem is to determine whether Athens ever had a viable democracy. There are two aspects of the problem. The first is to decide whether true democracy could exist when Athens had a slave population, when women were unable to exercise the franchise, when foreigners were unable to become citizens, and when the Athenians were willing to subjugate their allies and insist, even using brute force, that they remain within their empire. These limitations on Athenian democracy could provide a basis for the argument that there was no democracy at all.

[1] Carl Becker, *Modern Democracy* (New Haven, Conn.: Yale University Press, 1941), p. 33.
[2] The quotations from Thucydides, *History of the Peloponnesian War*, are from the translation by Richard Crawley in the edition published in New York by E. P. Dutton & Co., 1910.

But even if the system is accepted as a democracy, another aspect presents itself: Could it have existed without subsidy? Two major criticisms of Athenian democracy are that it depended for its existence on income from an empire and that slavery made possible the leisure for equal participation of its citizens.

It was the cornerstone of the democratization of the Athenian government that public officials (with few exceptions) should be selected by lot and that in the courts and Council as well as the Assembly the *demos* should do the work of government. For the poorest citizens to be able to participate, however, required that they be paid. The trend, during the fifth and fourth centuries, was always toward increased payment. William Scott Ferguson, in the selection from his important work on Greek imperialism, argues that democracy was unworkable without great expenditures of money and that for this money Athens required the imperial tribute and control of the seas. The empire was essential to the democracy, not a luxury or a needless evil, and if the empire paid in good measure so that Athens could be the school of Hellas, then the empire requires no apology.

There is a wide range of opinion about the extent and influence of slavery in Greece. Whether slavery was necessary to the democracy is a relevant question only if, like many economic historians, particularly those who see the over-all failure in terms of a class conflict, one accepts the extreme view that the Greeks based their civilization on slave labor. George Thomson, who takes that position, is an English historian and literary scholar who leans heavily on Marxist theory.

Both criticisms are countered by A. H. M. Jones, a leading Cambridge historian, who questions the contention that Athens was parasitic on its empire and on slavery. He analyzes the effects of these two institutions from an economic point of view. The reader may judge the validity of his arguments. One thing is certain: Jones's sympathy is with the democracy and his belief in it is optimistic—he is willing to forgive it its trespasses.

"Our constitution," said Pericles, "is called a democracy because power is in the hands not of a minority but the whole people." This deceptively simple statement embodies the theory of political equality which was intended to sustain Athenian democracy. Was this theory translated into action, or did the failure of Athenian democracy actually proceed from an initial failure to reconcile the theory with political reality?

The most straightforward analysis of the forces that militated against the success of the political ideal comes from J. B. Bury's famous *History of Greece*. In the first reading in the next section, he describes the growth of individualism and of capitalism and shows how and why these developments fostered values in conflict with the concept of political equality. The theory of political equality itself gave rise to demands for social and economic equality, but they were circumvented by a capitalist safeguard—the system of doles provided by the theoric fund.[3] One may reasonably ask if this "safeguard" was an early example of the "bread and circuses" formula of ancient Rome and, more important, if political democracy could exist when some form of economic democracy was lacking.

The other problem this raises is the extent to which the rich were exploited for the benefit of the poor. To many Greeks, within as well as outside Athens, democracy meant the rule of the poorest classes in their own interests. The unknown fifth-century critic referred to as the "Old Oligarch" summarized the oligarchic position (the attitude of the few as opposed to the many) in the first portion of his political pamphlet. Was he describing democracy? Or democrats in power?

When Pericles said "power is in the hands . . . of the whole people," he meant only the *citizens* of Athens, and he was himself responsible for a narrow definition of citizenship. Had the Athenians allowed the privileges of citizenship to be extended, according to F. W. Walbank, they might have achieved and transmitted a true democracy. Instead, the group he defines as a middle class insisted on controlling the franchise and thus inhibited the full evolution of democracy, which passed from a state of arrested development into decline. The core of his thesis is that democracy failed in the classical world because equality never penetrated far enough.

Precisely the opposite conclusion is reached by the historian M. Rostovtzeff. The difference between him and Walbank, in fact, is a clear illustration of the difficulties of being objective when dealing with issues that involve questions of value. Rostovtzeff considers the greatest weakness of Athenian democracy to have been its absolute insistence on quality. There is here an echo of Plato's criticism that democracy showered the blessings of equality on the equal and unequal alike. This insistence on equality, coupled with the idea that the state was the property of its citizens, conspired to level citizens downward to the lowest stratum of society. The end product of this levelling process was a tyranny which forced the rich to support the poor and found it necessary to limit freedom of speech. The death of Socrates, in this view, resulted from the ideal of equality, in the pejorative sense, fully realizing itself.

The arguments that center on the effectiveness of the political theory on which Athenian democracy was based lead directly to another group of arguments which begin with the premise that the causes for decline first revealed themselves in weaknesses and imperfections in the day-by-day operation of the constitution. There is no agreement among historians about precisely

---

[3] The theoric fund was established in the time of Pericles to provide public funds to poor citizens to pay for their seats at the theater; it was later used for other kinds of doles.

where responsibility should be placed for jamming and twisting the machinery of government so that it ceased to run democratically. Each of the theories urged, however, has won a sizable following. One of the most persistent arguments, presented by E. M. Walker in the *Cambridge Ancient History*, indicts the demagogues (or rabble-rousers) for exerting a bad influence on the Assembly and for being politically irresponsible. But to George Grote they were, as they claimed to be, the watchdogs of democracy, working to preserve it against its real enemies, the oligarchs. Grote, who served in the English Parliament in the nineteenth century, sees the demagogues as leaders of the opposition and a vital part of the democratic process.

Charles Alexander Robinson, Jr., following Thucydides, argues that it was not a particular group but the rule of one man that negated democracy. He reconstructs how it might have been possible for Pericles to take over in Athens so that what Thucydides wrote of him was true: "The power was really in the hands of the first citizen." Acceptance of the conclusion of Thucydides —and of Robinson—about Periclean Athens depends on an assessment of Thucydides' political leanings. This is done admirably in an article by a leading Canadian classicist, Malcolm F. McGregor, who also presents his own interpretation of the "rule" of Pericles.

In his *History*, Herodotus described a debate among the Persians on the nature of different forms of government. About a monarch, Herodotus wrote, "The worst of all is, that he sets aside the laws of the land. . . ." But what of the democracy? How did the people, given full legislative power, deal with their laws? In his trenchant analysis of the city-state in antiquity, Numa Denis Fustel de Coulanges emphatically dismisses "the singular error" that in city-states "men enjoyed liberty." His point is that without such liberty the name "democracy" meant little or nothing. Gustave Glotz, a modern French historian, takes the position that the Athenians worked out an equilibrium between liberty and the rule of law in the fifth century, but that in the fourth century the selfish interests of the democratic masses became predominant over the good of the state and the Athenians began ruling by caprice and decree. This absolutist tendency, apparent in the court and the Assembly, ultimately negated any claim that Athens was democratic. The Athenians would have done well to recall Sophocles' Chorus in *Antigone*:

> O fate of man, working both good and evil!
> When the laws are kept, how proudly his city stands!
> When the laws are broken, what of his city then?

Perhaps the Athenian failure will stand, after all, as the first and best illustration of Rousseau's assertion that "so perfect a form of government is not suited to mere men." In Athens, democracy exacted more from its citizens than it has ever done since. But if there is some homely wisdom in the notion that people get the government they deserve, it should be especially true of democracy. So the question needs to be reworded to read, not where did the ideal fail, but where did the people betray the ideal?

In Plato's dialogue *The Gorgias*, Socrates argued that if the people had chosen good leaders, they would have been improved by them. Pericles was a poor statesman and a poor choice if, as Socrates asserted, the people were in many ways worse after his tenure and if Pericles' reforms brought out their worst characteristics. The twentieth-century historian, John L. Myres, searching for the underlying causes of the shortcomings of the Athenians so evident in the fourth century, takes as his starting point three of the conditions Aristotle set down as indispensable if men are to be good and useful members of a state: breeding, training, and reasoning. After analyzing what each means and how it was dealt with, Myres concludes that the democracy failed because the Athenians themselves were found wanting on all three counts. Their "spiritual" impoverishment may have led inevitably to a bankruptcy of their political experiment. But in a wise and balanced summary of the many difficulties that finally destroyed democracy, T. R. Glover, one of the finest classicists of the twentieth century, emphasizes the agent that acted as a catalyst on the shortcomings of the Athenians—the Peloponnesian War. He argues that the war exposed the inabilities of the Athenians to deal with the disasters attendant on it, that it revealed their lack of foreign policy, and that it elicited the worst aspects of their individualism. And he adds a failing that the Greeks themselves—and Rousseau—would surely have understood: the war exposed their *hybris* (excessive pride).

Throughout it has been the historical problem of decline which has concerned us. As an epilogue, there is a brief selection by a prominent sociologist with a particular interest in political philosophy. Robert M. MacIver suggests that the history of democracy should be written as the evolution of an institution to which, at each stage, from first to last, something was added that has brought it closer to an ideal form. Was it, then, that in Athens the habit of democracy was not sufficiently ingrained? Or is it simply not possible to have a democracy perched on an undemocratic base—slavery, empire, and limited franchise? Or, perhaps, for all its imperfections and despite the gap between the ideal and the reality, Herodotus came closest to the heart of the matter when he wrote that "*demokratia*—the people ruling—even the name is beautiful."

HERBERT J. MULLER (1905–   ) is Distinguished
Service Professor of English and Government
at Indiana University. His interest in the story of
freedom is clearly evident in his recent books,
*Issues of Freedom, Freedom in the Ancient World,
Freedom in the Western World,* and *Freedom in the
Modern World.* Although Muller would surely agree
that the Athenians stand front and center in the
history of freedom and democracy, he points out that
it is altogether too easy to romanticize them. In
retrospect, even Athens' positive contributions may
be distorted by the awareness that something went
very wrong. Perhaps, as Muller writes in an
earlier passage in the book quoted here, "If we
remember that the Greeks were rather different from
their sculptured gods, we can better understand
their failures and better appreciate their triumphs."*

The Limitations of Greece

It is a mistaken piety that glosses over
the many embarrassing customs and convictions of the brilliant Greeks. Simply
as we value their way of life we need to
see clearly both their shortcomings and
their inherent limitations, the defects of
their virtues.

In the first place, these ancients were
very young, only a few centuries removed from barbarism. Their youthful-
ness is most apparent in the prehistoric
superstitions that were embedded in
their high culture as well as their folk-
ways, and which influenced their national life to an extent difficult for us to
realize. If the Athenians had lost the
battle of Marathon, they probably would
have become subjects of the Persians,
and never developed a Periclean Age;
yet Herodotus reports that they did not
begin this momentous battle until "the
victims showed themselves favorable."
and their chances were jeopardized by
the absence of the Spartans, who could
not march out of Sparta because the
moon had not yet reached the full. (It
appears that the course of history may
also be determined by the entrails of animals and the phases of the moon.)
Again, in the fatal campaign against
Syracuse, the turning point of the Peloponnesian War, the Athenian expedition was on the point of sailing home to
safety when an eclipse of the moon oc-

* From *The Uses of the Past* by Herbert J. Muller. Copyright 1952 by Oxford University Press,
Inc. Pp. 112–120 reprinted by permission.

curred, and their soothsayers prescribed a wait of thrice nine days; so the Athenians waited, to be utterly destroyed by the Syracusans.

Similarly the Greeks had little historical sense. The student of their history, Toynbee wrote, has the advantage of sitting through the whole play and listening to its beautifully articulate protagonists, who had "the wisdom of greater experience and the poignancy of greater suffering than ours." After such esthetic appreciation, however, the student had better discount and supplement this wisdom. The Greeks could only speculate about their early history because they had no records, no lists of kings, no dates, no chronology except for the Olympic games; when they grew critical of their traditional legends they had no ready means of substituting reliable knowledge, and surprisingly little interest in trying to get such knowledge. . . .

The Greeks were cribbed and cabined by their ideal of excellence. To follow for a moment Spengler's analysis of .the Classical spirit, they lived in a tidy Euclidean world, finite, static, complete. They had no feeling for horizons, prospects, or backgrounds, and no word for "space"; they had such a horror of infinity that the idea was virtually taboo. They had no desire to explore the whole world, to convert it, or to master it by technology. In their colonizing adventures they did not venture into the hinterlands or seek to establish a "new land"; their colonies clung to the Mediterranean, the mother-city, and the ancestral god. They had no Protestantism, no Romantic Movement, no stirring revolutions in art and thought; they had critics and reformers but no great rebels or missionaries consciously in advance of their time. They did not look to the future, or when they did they saw endless cycles, repetition rather than change. (They dropped Anaximander's theory of evolution.) They had so little interest even in keeping time that they were slow to make use of the clocks and calendars developed by Egypt and Babylonia. In general, their world was a world of forms, not of forces, and their main effort was to keep it small, clear, orderly, statuesque.

Spengler goes on to show how this effort shaped all the major creations of the Greek genius. Their political ideal was the well-ordered little *polis*, the state as statue. Their Olympian gods were superlative shapes, not omnipotent wills or superlative forces, and their mode of worship was a pious observance of forms, not a soaring aspiration. Their science was based on the concepts of matter and form, not of mass and energy; always true to form, Nature "abhorred a vacuum." Their mathematics was plane and solid geometry; they had no dynamics, no differential or infinitesimal calculus, no irrational numbers, no zero as a number. Their great ethical systems, such as the Stoic and Epicurean, alike held up an ideal of "statuesque steadiness"; their common aim was to limit rather than fulfil desire, to order rather than expand life. Their painting had no horizon or perspective, no sense of space or depth. Their architecture concentrated on the temple, the smallest of the great architectural forms, and to the end was based on the simple post and lintel. "Everything that is Classical," Spengler sums up, "is comprehensible in *one* glance." Greek culture has been so popular if only because it is the tidiest, most understandable of the great cultures.

As usual, Spengler ignores a great deal in order to keep this pattern neat. Like the classical scholars he derides, he falls into the error of identifying all Greece with its Apollonian ideal, slighting the strong Dionysian tendencies, the bold adventures in thought and political life, the restless, wilful spirit that led to endless war between classes and states. He becomes preposterous when he declares that "the Greeks willed nothing and dared nothing." Yet the Greek spirit was in fact considerably less daring and dynamic than the spirit of the Western world, which has sought to harness the forces of nature, searched out the subatomic world and the stellar universe, discovered new continents and "lands of opportunity," begot the idea of Progress, set off great revolutionary movements, sent out missionaries and crusaders—which has explored and exploited the whole world, and endeavored to make it over in its own image, whether of Christianity, democracy, capitalism, or communism. The Greeks accordingly avoided the excesses of this "Faustian" spirit, the penalties of a reach that exceeds a grasp; but they had to pay a price for their kind of perfection. Their failure was not merely a failure to realize their ideal—it was due as well to the limitations of this ideal.

Simplicity, clarity, perfection of form —these excellent qualities are not necessarily the supreme excellence, or the ultimate criteria of truth and beauty. They may sacrifice too much of the variety, complexity, fluidity, and ambiguity of human experience, the manifold possibilities of value; the deepest thought or the loftiest imagining is usually not the clearest. But the great danger that besets the classical ideal is classicism—its tendency to a static, sterile perfection. Although the Greek temple became a marvel of harmony and proportion, it had no future; its basic form of post and lintel was suitable only for small buildings; yet Greek architects clung to this simple form to the end. Hence the very perfections of the Greeks were bound to paralyze art and thought unless their admirers could recapture the spontaneous, adventurous spirit that had created the masterpieces. As it was, the classical spirit led to an excessive generality, a lifeless formalism, an artificial dignity, a rigid repose, a restraint that restrained no emotion to speak of. It led to the kind of classicism that we find in later Rome, and in Europe after the Renaissance, but also in the decline of Greece itself. For centuries Athens continued to admire itself as the "school of Hellas" while it rehearsed the old lessons, and failed to learn its own lesson. . . .

In this view, the enterprising, creative Greeks were not enterprising or creative enough. They were unequal to the challenge of their own achievements, or specifically to the new possibilities of tension, friction, and disorder created by their new ideal of freedom. If the immediate cause of their failure cause was the circumspection of the classical spirit. Behind their ideals of form and order lay a deep-seated fear of was the corruption of pride, a further cause was the circumspection of the classical spirit. Behind their ideals of form and order lay a deep-seated fear of change. Their typical way of adapting themselves to a world that kept changing in spite of them was the way of contemplation, of resignation, or of withdrawal. In this respect the Greeks were less proud and wilful than the Hebrews.

The Hebrews had a passion for justice on this earth, demanding the final establishment of terrestrial peace and order; the promises held up by their prophets were the fighting faith of their zealots. The Greeks could fight bravely for their city-state, but they had no such passion for the cause of justice or any ideal state on earth.

In other words, the freedom-loving Greeks lacked a deep faith in the power of freedom. While they conceived man as essentially a rational animal and believed that he could order his private life, they did not believe that he could progressively improve the collective life. They had little sense of history as creation or actual adventure, little confidence in man's ability to make his own history. Their ultimate principle remained Moira—a Fate to which the gods themselves were subject. Their greater writers usually asserted that this universal order was a rational, moral order, which punished *hubris*, but they often wrote as if it were a blind or hostile order; and in any case man could do nothing about it. He realized his rationality by contemplating or submitting to a given metaphysical order, not by seeking to create a new social order. This fatalism, which from the outset lay behind Greek thought, at the end dominated thought and paralyzed will. Moira became Tyche, or Chance.

All this is by no means to discredit the Greek genius. They were pioneers in the life of freedom, with no precedents to guide them, no settled democratic traditions to steady them. It is no wonder that their thought was conditioned by their social arrangements and reflected their limited knowledge and experience. The wonder remains that these fledglings dared and achieved so much. Say the worst about their political philosophy, and then one must add with Zimmern[1] that they made the all-important contribution to political philosophy—they invented it. Grant that their society was based on slavery, and that Aristotle defined a slave as an "animated instrument" who was "nothing of himself," it is much more remarkable that Euripides and other Greeks began to denounce this universal institution, which was accepted by Jesus and St. Paul centuries later, and still defended by Americans in the last century. In all fields of thought the Greeks took the necessary first steps. We are more knowing than they because we have had the privilege of knowing them, and the wit to carry on their pioneering adventure. My point, again, is simply that in justice both to them and to ourselves we need to see the Greeks as they were, taking full advantage of the perspectives afforded by our much wider experience and greater knowledge. We are unjust to Athens if we merely moralize about the sins of pride, forgetting the superstition, ignorance, immaturity, and provinciality that clouded its brilliance. . . .

[1] Alfred E. Zimmern, author of many works on Greek history, most notably *The Greek Commonwealth: Politics and Economics in Fifth Century Athens* (Oxford, 1911) .—*Ed.*

WILLIAM SCOTT FERGUSON (1875–1954) earned
his advanced degrees at Cornell University, and
taught at the University of California and at Harvard,
where, in 1912, he became the first professor of
ancient history. Among his chief works are *Hellenistic
Athens, Treasures of Athens,* and *Athenian Tribal
Cycles.* His study of *Greek Imperialism* remains
a classic work on the subject. Athenian imperialism
seems to him a reconciliation between the imperial
idea and the self-governing city-state; Athens,
when it was called an empire, ruled what was basically
an aggregate of separate political units, all of
them Greek. Democracy no less than kingship can
find justification for pursuing an imperial policy, and
Ferguson explains why this policy appeared to
be a necessity to the Athenian democracy.*

Athens: An Imperial Democracy

There never was a people which made
the principle that all its citizens were
equal a more live reality than the Athenians made it; and no state to my
knowledge was more cunningly con-
trived to insure the government of the
people than was theirs. Yet they became
imperialists with ardor and conviction,
and with this much of logical consequence, that, while they believed in democracy for everybody, they did not
doubt that the Athenians had earned
the right to rule both Greeks and barbarians by the acquisition of superior
culture. Equality among its citizens
Athens carefully distinguished from
equality among all men.

The foundations of Athenian democracy and empire were laid by Themistocles, whose figure moves weird and
gigantic through the golden mist in
which Herodotus has enveloped the
great Persian War. And it was this gen-
ial statesman, to whose unerring skill
in discerning the course of coming
events the austere historian Thucydides
pays a rare tribute, who mapped out
for his city the foreign policy by which
it had the best chance of realizing its
imperial ambition. Let it use its great
fleet, which by fifteen years of persistent
advocacy he had led the Athenians to
build, as its arm of offense, and its im-
pregnable walls, which he had enabled

---

* From *Greek Imperialism* by William Scott Ferguson (Boston, 1913) pp. 39–44; 61–74. Copyright by Houghton Mifflin Company. Reprinted by permission.

the Athenians to construct despite the treacherous opposition of Sparta, as a bulwark of defense and a basis for timely advance against its powerful continental rivals. Let it utilize the wave of democratic fervor then sweeping through Greece to consolidate its power within the Confederacy of Delos and to undermine and eventually to overthrow the leadership which Sparta, by the support of dying mediaeval aristocracies, had hitherto possessed in Hellenic affairs. Let it make peace on advantageous terms with Persia; use the liberty thus secured to break the power of Sparta, and, on the basis of a consolidated Hellas, strike boldly for Athenian dominion of the world.

It seems almost incredible that a clear-headed man should have entertained a programme of such magnitude. But we must remember that never had human beings more clearly performed the obviously miraculous. *We* know, on the authority of a German military expert, that, had the host which followed Xerxes to Athens numbered the 5,283,220 men attributed to it by Herodotus "without taking count of women cooks, concubines, eunuchs, beasts of burden, cattle, and Indian dogs," its rear guard must have been still filing out of Sardis while its van was vainly storming Thermopylae. But what Herodotus reports is what the Athenians believed. They had met and routed the might of all Asia. They had mastered in fair fight the conquerors of all other peoples. The world was theirs: it was merely a question of taking possession.

Themistocles had, accordingly, to reckon with a national self-confidence which knew no bounds. And this had been increased by famous victories of Cimon over the Persians, and a revolt

of the Helots which disclosed the fatal weakness of Sparta, when in 461 B.C. the task of conducting the fierce current of national energy, first for fifteen years (461–446 B.C.) in a heroic, but fruitless, struggle by sea and land against the Greeks and Persians simultaneously, and then for fifteen further years (446–431 B.C.) in the prosecution of glorious works of peace, fell upon the broad shoulders of Pericles, Xanthippus's son.

It is conceded that there is no taskmaster so ruthless as one's own will. The impulse to action during this strenuous epoch came from the Athenian people itself, not from its chief statesman. That fact does not, however, diminish the credit of Pericles. The golden age of Greece is, properly speaking, a golden age of Athens, and to its birth many things contributed; but decisive among them, in addition to the intensity of national life already alluded to, was an unrivaled facility for great leaders to get into effective contact with the masses under conditions in which there was the fullest opportunity for men in general to use their natural powers to the utmost. This happy combination of creative genius and receptive multitude arose in the main from the democratic institutions of Athens; but, for the public and private wealth without which Athenian democracy proved unworkable, and for the imaginative stimulus which enterprises of great pitch and moment alone give, the possession of empire was, perhaps, essential.

In the age of Pericles, Athens was a city with a population of about 150,000. Attica, the territory of the Athenians, had an approximately equal number of inhabitants. Of the 300,000 thus accounted for, about one third was servile and one sixth foreign. The free and franchised population made up one half of the total, and yielded about 50,000 males of military age.

The empire of the Athenians consisted of five provinces, the Thracian, Hellespontine, Insular, Ionian, and Carian, with a total population of perhaps 2,000,000. It formed a complex of islands, peninsulas, and estuaries, the most remote extremities of which were distant two hundred or two hundred and fifty miles from Athens. The highways of this empire were the land-locked channels and lakes which make up the Aegean Archipelago. Their greatest length in normal circumstances was a continuous voyage of about eight days. On the other hand, no land way of more than a single day's march need be traversed by an Athenian expedition aimed at any of its subject cities. Without the control of the sea the empire was, accordingly, unthinkable. This absent, the district fell at once into more than four hundred fragments, the thousand "cities" from which, according to the comedian Aristophanes, the Athenians gathered tribute.

The Athenian sphere of naval operations and of political and commercial interests reached far beyond the frontiers of the empire. It included points like Sicily, Egypt, Phoenicia, and the Euxine, distant over six hundred miles from the Piraeus. An Athenian fleet might thus require the best part of a month to reach its destination. The world which had to take careful account of the Athenian naval power in all its political and military calculations, the world which Athens under Pericles sought to dominate, must have had a population of over 20,000,000.

If, then, we take into account the ratio of dominant, subject, and foreign elements, and also the time consumed in reaching with ships, orders, or explanations, the outer limits of authority, the magnitude of Athens's imperial undertaking will stand comparison with that of England in modern times.

In Sparta the gravestone of a citizen was inscribed regularly with his name alone. No epitaph was needed there to tell the tale of a life; for the life of one citizen was the well-known life of all. If, however, a man had died for his country, two words, . . . "in war," expressed with laconic brevity his ground of distinction.

For those who fell in battle Athens set apart a public cemetery near the Dipylon Gate, and at the end of every campaign a commemorative service was held there in honor of the year's crop of martyrs. A man high in public esteem voiced the nation's gratitude for the sacrifice. On such an occasion, at the end of the first year of the Peloponnesian War, Pericles reversed the normal procedure, and, instead of expatiating on the merits of the fallen, he explained in an eloquent speech why Athens was worthy of loyalty unto death. Thucydides heard his words, and, perhaps many years afterwards, reproduced them as best he could in the famous *Funeral Oration*.

The statesman did not linger long over the legendary glories of Athens. Her alleged boons to humanity—grain, the norms of civilized life, the drama; the services, that is to say, upon which the later Athenians dwelt with special pride—had no meaning for him. Two things their ancestors had done: they had defended their country successfully, and had transmitted to their descend-

ants a free state. "And if these were
worthy of praise," proceeds his splendid
exordium, "still more were our fathers,
who added to their inheritance, and
after many a struggle transmitted to us
their sons this great empire." . . .

There is nothing that dies so hard as
a well-nurtured delusion. In the ro-
mantic-idealizing view of the Greeks
which was long current, the Athenians
found leisure for art, literature, and philosophy by having all their work done
for them by their slaves. By this means,
too, they were enabled to devote themselves freely to politics. If this were so,
the inference of Calhoun was a sound
one, that seen "in its true light" slavery
was "the most safe and stable basis for
free institutions in the world." The
"first lie" is that the Athenians of the
great age, whose dominant characteristic
was their vibrant mental and physical
activity, were in any sense men of leisure. The few among them who had
slaves and other property to the extent
of great wealth had to make and manage their own investments. The majority
of the farmers had to till the land
with their own hands. Many citizens—
at least one third of the whole, in all
probability—had to earn their living by
selling their labor. This they could do
easily in the time of the empire. For
during that period of rapid commercial
and industrial expansion the demand
for labor was so great that the price
could be regulated only by the constant
import of slaves and by a steady stream
of immigration from less prosperous
parts of Greece. Outside labor served the
purpose in Athens which immigrant
labor serves in the United States to-day.
With its growth grew the need that the
material prosperity which occasioned it
should endure. The problem of food-

supply became progressively acute and
the control of the sea was soon seen to
be an economic necessity. More than one
half of the grain sold on the Athenian
market came ultimately from abroad, as
did an even larger proportion of the
raw materials of Athenian industry.
"The Athenians are the only people in
the Hellenic and barbarian world,"
wrote an Athenian aristocrat in about
420 B.C., "who are able to control an
abundant supply of raw materials. For
if a state is rich in timber for ship-
building, where will it find a market for
it if not with the masters of the sea? If
another abounds in iron or bronze or
linen yarn, where will it find a market
except with the sea-lord? Yet this is the
stock from which ships are made in
Athens. One city yields timber to her,
another iron, a third bronze, a fourth
linen yarn, a fifth wax, and so on. Moreover, Athens prevents her rivals from
transporting goods to other countries
than Attica by the threat of driving
them from the sea altogether."

The demands put upon the time of
Athenian citizens by the state were
enormous, but not such as to cripple
economic production. A comparison
with modern conditions will make this
clear. A little less frequently than once a
week the ecclesia [Assembly] met, but
the attendance was generally less than
one tenth of those qualified. That represents a suspension of work roughly
equivalent to our Saturday afternoons
and legal holidays. A little oftener than
once a week a contest or other public
festival occurred, and to these there was,
it seems, a pretty general resort. They
correspond to our fair-days and Sundays.
Preparation for the contests was, perhaps, not more destructive of money-
earning time than are our collegiate and

university courses. During their nine-teenth and twentieth years young Athe-nians of the upper third trained for the army; but it was not till a century after Pericles's death that universal military service for a similar period was made compulsory—as in modern Europe. We may assume that at least two years of every citizen's life was required for de-liberative and administrative work; and, having regard to the imperial service, we may, perhaps, advance this require-ment to three. That is an enormous en-largement of modern demands. The same ratio would give the United States two million and a half or three million public employees, exclusive of postmas-ters and postal clerks, tax-collectors, and day laborers of every description. But a bald comparison of this sort is mislead-ing. Athens regularly employed a com-mittee of ten to do one man's work, with the result that all of them were free to give nine tenths of their time to their private business. The council during the year and the jury courts at its expiry were there to insure the state that, even if his colleagues would let him, any par-ticular official did not neglect his pub-lic duties. Nor was the Athenian prac-tice wildly extravagant so long as the magistrate received, not a living salary, but an indemnity equal only to a com-mon workman's daily wage. The Athe-nians employed four hundred or even two thousand jurors where we employ twelve; but they had neither high sal-aried judges nor exacting lawyers to pay, since the judicial system worked without either. The juryman's fee, moreover, was a meagre indemnity, com-parable to the old-age pension paid in the progressive countries of modern Eu-rope.

The payment of indemnities for serv-ice in the council, the magistracies, the jury courts, and for attendance in the theatre, music-hall, and stadion, was a Periclean innovation. He did not in-tend to create a class of salaried officials; nor yet to make an advance toward com-munism. His ideal was political, not eco-nomic, equality—to enable all, irrespec-tive of wealth or station, to use the opportunities and face the obligations which democracy brought in its train. Like all the great democratic leaders who preceded him, he was a nobleman by birth and breeding, and, like them, he did not doubt for a moment that the culture which ennobled the life of his class would dignify and uplift that of the masses also. To give the working-man the political insight and knowledge of the Eupatrids;[1] to lend to him the grace and elasticity of movement which physical culture gave them; to fill his memory with the noble thoughts set in melodious and stirring words which they got from their intimacy with great po-etry; to inspire in him, though a mere artisan, an artist's taste and fervor for formal beauty—that was to bless him with more than leisure. It was to unite the whole people in a community of high ideas and emotions. It was to make them a nation of noblemen. We do not wonder much that in the furtherance of this cause the men of large wealth in Athens volunteered to assume in turn financial and personal responsibility for the support of the theatre, the opera-house, the stadion, and the gymnasia. It was a heavy burden, but, in the absence of a regular property or income tax, generosity became at once a duty and a wise precaution.

[1] The old landed nobility at Athens; literally, the well-born.—*Ed*.

A nation of noblemen is a luxury for which somebody has to pay. Athens, in Pericles's memorable phrase, was "the school of Hellas." It was right, he thought, that the Hellenes should sacrifice something for their education. He had tried to make them all contributory allies of Athens, but had failed in the attempt. As a good schoolmaster he was determined, none the less, to hold those "well in hand" whom he had under his care.

The physical means to this end was the control of the sea. The advantages of sea power in warfare, in enabling the holder of it to circumscribe according to his convenience the area of military action, as well as in facilitating mobilization, transport, and communications, were not perceived for the first time by the English Admiralty, much less by Clausewitz and Captain Mahan. They are stated in the clearest terms by a contemporary of Pericles.[2] Here is what he says: "The subjects of a power which is dominant by land have it open to them to form contingents from several small states and to muster in force to battle. But with the subjects of a naval power it is different. As far as they are groups of islands (and the whole world, we may remark in passing, is now simply a magnified Aegean Archipelago) it is impossible for their states to meet together for united action, for the sea lies between them, and the dominant power is master of the sea. And even if it were possible for them to assemble in some single island unobserved, they would only do so to perish of famine. And as to the states subject to Athens which are not islanders, but situated on the continent, the larger are held in check by need and the small ones absolutely by fear, since there is no state in existence which does not depend upon imports and exports and these she will forfeit, if she does not lend a willing ear to those who are masters of the sea. In the next place, a power dominant by sea can do certain things which a land power is debarred from doing; as, for instance, ravage the territory of a superior, since it is always possible to coast along to some point, where either there is no hostile force to deal with or merely a small body; and in case of an advance in force on the part of the enemy they can take to their ships and sail away. Such a performance is attended by less difficulty than that experienced by the army marching along the seaboard to the rescue. Again, it is open to a power so dominating by sea to leave its own territory and sail off on as long a voyage as you please. . . . There is just one thing which the Athenians lack. Supposing they were the inhabitants of an island, and were still, as now, rulers of the sea, they would have had it in their power to work whatever mischief they liked and suffer no evil in return."

At all costs Athens must retain control of the sea. That meant to keep the fleet constantly in fighting trim. In the effort the Athenians made the most heroic financial and personal sacrifices, demonstrating clearly that popular government need not be self-indulgent. Neither the aristocracy in England nor Napoleon in France was as hard a taskmaster of the people as the majority which ruled in Athens. Between 410 and 402 B.C.—a time of great economic distress—a well-to-do citizen was called

[2] Pseudo-Xenophon, *State of the Athenians*, II, 2 ff. The unknown author is now more commonly identified as the "Old Oligarch," which accurately denotes his political point of view.—Ed.

upon to expend twenty thousand franks [sic]—which are perhaps equal in purchasing power to as many dollars—on what we may call national education and entertainment. His taxes on the account of the fleet amounted in the same years to double as much, or forty-three thousand franks. Great as was the burden of the rich, that of the commons was conceded by their adversaries to have been still greater. "In the first place," writes an aristocrat in about 420 B.C.,[3] "it is only just that the poorer classes and the 'people' of Athens should have the advantage over the men of birth and wealth, seeing that it is the people who man the fleet and put round the city her girdle of power. The steersman, the boatswain, the lieutenant, the look-out-man at the prow, the shipwright—these are the people who engird the city with power far rather than her heavy infantry and men of birth and quality." Plutarch tells us that on a peace footing Athens kept a fleet of sixty ships on the sea for eight months of every year. To man such a squadron 10,200 rowers, 480 officers, and 600 marines would be required.[4] In other words, one quarter of all the citizens of Athens would have lived on their battleships for three quarters of every year. We might believe this report, if it were not contradicted by Aristotle, who in a place, where exaggeration, not reduction, is suspected, makes the fleet of Athens, which was constantly in service in time of war, consist only of twenty guardships. Hence one twelfth and not one quarter of all the Athenians were on active naval duty during the sailing season of almost every year. In addition, two thousand men were drafted yearly by lot to serve in garrisons throughout the empire; so that, if these are added to the seven hundred (?) imperial magistrates, and the five hundred guards of the arsenals, nearly another one twelfth of the citizens was involved.

This computation takes no account of the demands of naval warfare. In the Athenian dockyards lay ready for action four hundred battleships, from which the requisite number was selected for each particular expedition. If two hundred and fifty vessels were mobilized, as occasionally happened, nearly fifty thousand additional sailors were required. With the use of every possible citizen Athens could not produce such a number. She commonly did her utmost and called upon the allies for the rest.

It is true that tribute was collected from the allies to enable Athens to build the ships and pay the sailors; but it is also true that, in addition, huge sums were contributed for mobilization expenses by rich Athenians and were advanced for heavy war expenses by the Athenian treasury. And Athens gave freely not only of her money but also of her blood. The death roll of one of the ten corps into which the Athenians were divided for army and navy purposes is extant for the year 459 B.C. "Of the Erechtheid *phyle*," it runs, "these are they who died in the war, in Cyprus, in Egypt, in Phoenicia, at Halieis, in Aegina, at Megara, in the same year"; and one hundred and seventy-two names follow. It was not the year of a great battle, or of an Athenian disaster, yet in it the death rate must have been nearly twice as great as the birth rate;

---

[3] *Ibid.*, 2.

[4] "The core of the rowing crews was the lowest class of citizens, those who couldn't afford to equip themselves as soldiers. The rest simply had to be hired. . . ." Quoted from Lionel Casson, *The Ancient Mariners* (New York, 1959), p. 96. —Ed.

so costly in lives was the empire to its lords in war-time.

On three specific points and on one general ground, contemporaries both within and without Athens assailed the treatment accorded by the Periclean democracy to its subjects. In no instance, however, is the charge of misbehavior established conclusively, though in this matter, as in so many others in the history of Greece, our judgment is dependent upon the point at which we transfer our sympathy from the city-states, which were the bearers of culture in the Greek Middle Ages, to the whole people, for whose progress and independence urban particularism was finally fatal. "Surely Hellas is insulted with a dire insult," declared the opponents of Pericles,[5] "and manifestly subjected to tyranny when she sees that, with her own enforced contributions for the war, we are gilding and bedizening our city, which, for all the world like a wanton woman, adds to her wardrobe precious stones and costly statues and temples worth their millions." To this accusation the proper retort was, not that having provided adequate protection against Persia, Athens was free to spend the money contributed by the subjects in any way she pleased; for the logical inference was then that the contributions were excessive. Pericles may not have cared to be logical, but he could not ignore forms. Had he been able to show, as has been claimed recently, that he used for building purposes only the sixtieth of the tribute, which had been dedicated as the first fruits to Athena, he would never have been attacked at all. Evidently, he spent on Athenian

[5] Plutarch, *Pericles*, 12. (Translated by Perrin.)

public works much larger sums derived indirectly from the tribute, for which course the defense actually made seems to have been that the money was due Athens for losses sustained during the invasion of Xerxes and for sums advanced to the war fund during the continuance of the struggle with Persia. In any case the tribute paid was a mere bagatelle as compared with what the subjects saved through having no fleets of their own to maintain.

The charge is more serious that in order to enjoy "the steady receipt of salaries throughout the year derived from the court fees"; to "manage the affairs of the subjects while seated at home without the expense of naval expeditions"; to "preserve the partisans of democracy and ruin its opponents"; to boost the business of hotel keepers and such ilk in Athens, and to win for the common citizens the flattery and consideration that would be shown otherwise only to generals and ambassadors, the Athenians "compelled the allies to voyage to Athens in order to have their cases tried." For it seems clear that the law courts at Athens were usually so clogged with litigation that the gain in having a model code of law and in escaping the fierce partisanship of the local tribunals was largely neutralized by the added expense and humiliation. The real justification of the practice was that it obviated the necessity of sending out naval expeditions.

In the third place Athens took from the allies lands and settled them with impecunious Athenians; but in payment therefor reductions of tribute were given. On the other hand, thousands from the allied cities migrated to Athens, and, while not escaping military or financial service, or obtaining Athenian citizenship, they were cordially welcomed, and enjoyed to the full the commercial and industrial advantages of the metropolis. Again, Athenians often found it less profitable to invest capital in Attic land, which was exposed to hostile attack, than in lands on the islands of the empire, which the fleet protected. Hence there were many Attic farmers in the subject territory, their right to own foreign real estate being secured by commercial treaties. There was accordingly economic give and take, the military preponderance of Athens being, however, responsible for the result that the Athenians abroad were often policemen, the allies in Athens, hostages.

In all three instances of alleged misbehavior, it must be admitted that the defense offered by the Athenian apologists simply added insult to injury in the view of a majority of the subjects. But for them Athens, arrogant or conciliatory, malefactor or benefactor, was always a foreign governor to be gotten rid of at any cost. Such uncompromising sentiments time alone could alter, and to secure the benefits of time Pericles endeavored to avoid an Hellenic war. His policy of peace after 446 B.C. was, therefore, the sound policy of an imperialist.

The general ground on which contemporaries criticized the Athenian régime was that under it every assistance was given by the state to the least cultivated portion of the inhabitants both of Athens and of its four hundred and twenty subject cities, at the expense of the most intelligent and cultivated elements; that the highest goal of endeavor was moral and intellectual mediocrity. There may be some truth in this contention. The case would be more conclusive, however, if the tendency of the critics to identify intelligence with wealth and cultivation with birth were less obvious. If the point be granted, we must accept the opinion of those historians who affirm that Athens was great in this age despite, and not because of, its democracy. Personally, I do not believe that this was so. I cannot admit that extirpation of the best was practiced in an age in which ideas were created and forms were perfected for their literary and artistic expression which have been the wonder and despair of the men of the highest cultivation from that day to this. Does it not seem like irony that a régime is charged with promoting mediocrity under which rose Sophocles, Herodotus, Phidias, Pericles, Euripides, Hippocrates, Socrates, and Thucydides? Much more important than the leveling tendency of the democracy was the facility it afforded for men of ability both to rise to the top and to find there a sympathetic and critical audience. So much for democracy.

The existence of slavery in democratic Athens is an embarrassment to those historians who prefer to concentrate on the virtues of Athenian democracy. Still, there it was, and the issue is how necessary it may have been to the existence of democracy. The answer depends in part on the extent to which Greek society in general appears to have been economically dependent on its slaves. GEORGE THOMSON (1903–) presents the case for Greece as a slave society. Thomson was educated at Cambridge University and except for one year was a Fellow of King's College, Cambridge, from 1927–1936; he has been professor of Greek history at the University of Birmingham since 1937. His published works include *Aeschylus and Athens, Marxism and Poetry,* and *Studies in Ancient Greek Society,* vol. I, *The Prehistoric Aegean.**

Slavery in Ancient Greece

The two centuries preceding the Persian Wars saw the introduction of the sheep-shears, rotary quern, wine-press, and crane. After them no further inventions are recorded before the Hellenistic age. Thus, in industrial as well as commercial progress the fifth century was a turning-point. What was it that brought the movement to a stop? The answer is that this was the century in which "slavery seized on production in earnest."

In general, the slave had no incentive to increase production, because the whole of his surplus product was taken from him. On the other hand, so long as the supply was plentiful, he could be worked to death, like the African miner today. His cost of reproduction was less than that of the free labourer. His labour power was unskilled but cheap. It was profitable, but only at a low level of production. Moreover, being overworked, short-lived and deprived of family life, he was not in a position to acquire or transmit any skill, even if he had been encouraged to do so; and hence slave labour obstructed the improvement of technique. Freemen had no interest in combining with slaves against their common exploiters; rather, their aim was to buy slaves of their own,

* From George Thomson, *Studies in Ancient Greek Society,* vol. II, *The First Philosophers* (London: Lawrence & Wishart, 1955), pp. 196–205. Reprinted by permission of Lawrence & Wishart, Ltd., and The Citadel Press.

and this they could hope to do, so long as they were cheap. The main source of supply was kidnapping and conquest. Thus, besides preventing the increase of wealth, slavery promoted its destruction through internecine wars, in which Greek enslaved Greek. In these circumstances it became expedient to kill the adult males because, being trained to arms, they were difficult to manage, and keep only the women and children. This practice was well established in the fifth century B.C.

In spite of these considerations, some historians, anxious to present "the glory that was Greece" in the most favourable light, have discounted the part played by slave labour and even declared that "Greek society was not a slave society." In order to test such statements it is enough to turn the pages of Herodotus and Thucydides.

Of the Greek words for "slave," some were used loosely, but one had a very definite meaning. The word *andrápodon,* "chattel slave," means literally a "man-footed" creature, being formed on the analogy of *tetrápoda,* "four-footed" cattle. . . . In all the passages that follow the reference is to *andrápoda,* that is, to chattel slaves.

The word occurs for the first time in the *Iliad,* where Euneos of Lemnos offers wine in exchange for metals, oxen, hides, and slaves. . . . The slaves sold at Kyzikos were *andrápoda.* . . . The first Greek city to employ chattel slaves was Chios, where there was a slave market throughout antiquity, and it is noteworthy that as early as 600 B.C. the constitution of this island was democratic. About the same time Periandros, tyrant of Corinth, sent 300 young men from Kerkyra, a Corinthian colony, to Sardeis, where they were to be castrated

and serve as eunuchs. A century later we hear, again from Chios, of one Panionios, who made a handsome fortune by procuring good-looking Greek boys, castrating them, and selling them at Ephesos and Sardeis. The people of Arisbe, one of the six original cities of Lesbos, were enslaved by their neighbours of Methymna. Some prisoners from Lesbos were employed in chain gangs by Polykrates, tyrant of Samos, on the fortification of the island. A band of emigrants from Samos, who had settled in Crete, were attacked by the inhabitants together with some seamen from Aigina and enslaved. One of the inducements offered to the Persians for subjugating Naxos, which was then under a democracy, was that the island had a large slave population. When the Persians conquered Ionia the citizens of Samos sailed away to Sicily, where they seized the Greek city of Zankle. This they did with the support of Hippokrates, tyrant of Gela, who in return for his assistance took half the slave population, together with the majority of the citizens, for work in his chain gangs. When the Persians invaded Greece, they were under orders to enslave the inhabitants of Eretria and Athens and dispatch them to Sousa. They were able to carry out the order in respect of the Eretrians, who were eventually settled near the Persian capital; but the Athenians eluded them. It seems that even at this period there already existed in Anatolia large landed estates worked by slave labour; for, when Xerxes entered Phrygia at the head of his army, he was entertained by one Pythios, reputed to be the wealthiest of his subjects, who bestowed on him vast sums in gold and silver, adding that he still had plenty to live on from his farms and slaves.

Following up the victory over Persia, the Athenians captured Eion in Thrace and sold the inhabitants into slavery; then they sailed to Skyros, enslaved the inhabitants, and replaced them with planters from Athens. Meanwhile Gelon, tyrant of Syracuse, had kidnapped the common people of Megara Hyblaia and Euboia, two Greek colonies in Sicily, and sold them for export. In 430 B.C., at the outbreak of the Peloponnesian War, the Athenians captured Argos Amphilochikon and sold the inhabitants into slavery. In 427 B.C. the Thebans stormed the neighbouring city of Plataiai, executed 200 of the men, and enslaved the women and children. In 425 B.C. the democrats of Kerkyra massacred the oligarchs and enslaved their women and children. In 421 B.C. the Athenians captured Torone and Skione. At Torone they dispatched the men to Athens and enslaved the women and children, at Skione they massacred the men, enslaved the women and children, and resettled the territory with planters from Plataiai. In 416 B.C. they subjugated Melos, massacred the men, enslaved the women and children, and resettled the island with planters from Athens. During the campaign in Sicily an Athenian squadron sailing along the north coast put in at Hykkara, kidnapped the inhabitants, and sold them at Katane. After the rout of the Athenians, not less than 7000 prisoners, Athenians and their allies, were thrown into the quarries, where many of them perished, and the survivors were sold into slavery.

These are cases of Greeks enslaving Greeks. Of the regular traffic in barbarians the ancient writers tell us almost nothing, simply taking it for granted; but we learn from Aristophanes and other Attic sources of his time that the slave population of Athens was drawn from countries as distant as Illyria, Thrace, Scythia, the Caucasus, Cappadocia, Phrygia, Lydia, Caria, Syria, Egypt, and Arabia. As to prices, the best evidence is an inscription of the year 414 B.C., from which we learn that sixteen slaves belonging to a resident alien were sold by auction at prices ranging from 70 to 301 *drachmai*, with an average of 168 *dr.* for males and 147½ *dr.* for females. These sums may be compared with the fees paid to professional teachers for tutoring the sons of the well-to-do. Euenos of Paros offered a course on "human and political virtue" for what was regarded as the very modest fee of 500 *dr.*

From this it is clear that in the period under review there was a continuous demand for slave labour. We do not know the size of the slave population. All we can say is that at Athens it seems to have risen sharply during the latter half of the fifth century. Thus Thucydides relates that in the year 458–457 B.C., when the Athenians decided to fortify the city in circumstances that demanded the utmost speed, the whole people turned out on the job, including women and children. He does not mention slaves, as he might be expected to have done, if they had been available in large numbers. The same author records that in 413 B.C. over 20,000 slaves deserted to the Spartans, who had occupied Dekeleia, most of them being manual workers. It may be inferred that they had been employed in the quarries and mines. We know that in this generation Nikias, leader of the ill-fated Sicilian expedition, owned 1000 slaves, whom he hired out for work in the mines at an annual return of about 10 talents. Assuming that he had bought them at an average price of 168 *dr.* per head (a figure which may well be too high, since only the cheapest slaves would be sent to the mines), it may be reckoned that he received an annual return of at least 35 percent. So high a return in this field of investment must have tended to maintain high rates of interest in general. It was evidently a common thing for those who owned only a few slaves to employ them in this way, receiving from each a return of an obol or more a day. Apart from the mines, the largest concentration we hear of at Athens is the arms factory of Kephalos, who employed 120 slaves. This was no doubt exceptional. A generation later we hear of a well-to-do family whose property consisted of a house in town, two country farms, and a cobbler's shop employing ten or eleven slaves. Large numbers of slaves were employed in domestic service and also in brothels. Glotz has estimated than an ordinary Athenian household might contain from three to twelve slaves. This is no more than a guess, but it is important to note that even the poorer citizens seem to have had one or two slaves. Chremylos, in the *Wealth* of Aristophanes, is a poor peasant; yet he owns several slaves.[1] Slaves and poor citizens were employed in the same conditions on public works. The extent to which slave labour had encroached on free labour at Athens by the end of the fifth century may be judged from the accounts for the Erechtheion, which was built in 408 B.C. Of the seventy-one men engaged on the job, sixteen were slaves, thirty-five were resident aliens, and twenty were citizens. The reason why the third figure is so low is of course that the citizens enjoyed the franchise, which entitled them to earn money as jurors, to partake of the meat and wine which was distributed free at the frequent public festivals, and to put their names down in the lotteries for colonial plantations. They were protected to some extent by democracy.

What then is our conclusion? Ehrenberg writes as follows:

> The question of free and slave labour is really the question of manufacturing on a small or on a large scale. Since we do not believe in the predominant economic importance of big *ergastéria*, where slave labour was generally preferred, we do not believe in the predominant role of slave labour in general. It was necessary and needed everywhere, but rather as supplementary and not as part of the foundations of economic life. Free men never felt slave labour as a danger, hardly ever as a disadvantage.

In support of this view he appeals to Westermann, whom he describes as "the outstanding living expert on all questions of Greek slavery":[2]

> The slaves were employed at the same work as the free, usually side by side with them and apparently without prejudice or friction. In any sense which implies either that the enslaved population predominated over the free or that the Greek city-states displayed the mentality of a slave-ridden

---

[1] Even in Hesiod, the small farmer's minimum equipment includes a slave woman (*Op.* 405–406). The testimony of Aristophanes is discounted by A. H. M. Jones on the ground that "comedy was after all written by well-to-do authors, and slaves provided a variety of comic turns." It might be added that modern accounts of ancient Athens are "after all" the work of well-to-do historians. Besides reducing Aristophanes to the level of a music-hall comedian, Jones has overlooked the fact that Chremylos owns a number of slaves in addition to the one who does duty on the stage.

[2] William L. Westermann, now deceased, was the author of *The Slave Systems of Greek and Roman Antiquity* (Philadelphia, 1955), and many articles on slavery.—*Ed.*

society, Greek society was not founded on slavery.

There is an axiom of political economy which these scholars have overlooked:

If it is a scientific task to resolve the outward and visible movement into the inward and actual movement, it stands to reason that the conceptions regarding the laws of production which the agents of production and circulation form in their heads will differ widely from the real laws, being merely the conscious expression of the apparent movements.[3]

The Athenian citizens felt no danger or even disadvantage in slave labour, so long as they could exploit it directly or indirectly by the methods mentioned above; and that is what they did. In the fourth century they became a class of *rentiers* living on their unearned income and despising manual labour as an occupation fit only for barbarians and slaves. Of course, they were not conscious of this mentality as slave-ridden; on the contrary, they appealed to the self-evident truth that, since the slave was inferior by nature, it was in his own interest to be treated as a slave. This, like similar sophistries put forward by white settlers and their descendants in Africa and America today, was "merely

the conscious expression of the apparent movement," and proves nothing except the capacity of an exploiting class to deceive itself.

If we set aside these ideological factors and turn to the objective relations of production, what remains of Ehrenberg's argument? Simply this: the Athenian economy was based on small-scale production, and therefore slave labour cannot have played a large part in it. The fallacy is obvious.

The truth is that, just because they were based on small-scale production, the Greek city-states, having grown up in conformity with the new developments in the productive forces, especially iron-working and the coinage, were able, under the democracy, to insinuate slave labour surreptitiously into all branches of production, and so create the illusion that it was something ordained by nature. It was then that "slavery seized on production in earnest." This was the culminating point in the evolution of ancient society, to be followed by a long decline, in which the limitations inherent in a slave economy asserted themselves on an ever-increasing scale, obstructing the further development of the productive forces and diverting the energies of society from the exploitation of nature to the exploitation of man.

[3] Marx C 3. 369 (Karl Marx, *Capital*).

By tracing the economic background of Athenian
democracy both during and after the period when
Athens received the greatest returns from its empire,
A. H. M. JONES (1904–   ) draws the teeth from
the argument that the democracy could not exist
without imperial tribute. He also refutes Thomson's
thesis that Greek society was dependent on slavery.
In an article titled "The Athenian Democracy and
Its Critics," he summarizes his over-all attitude
toward democracy. "My readers can judge," he writes,
"whether the 'extreme democracy,' in which the
people were sovereign, and vulgar persons who worked
with their hands enjoyed full political rights . . .
was indeed so pernicious a form of government
as Athenian philosophers and historians represent."
Jones is professor of ancient history at Cambridge
University, and is the author, among other works,
of *The Greek City from Alexander to Justinian,
Ancient Economic History, Athens of Demosthenes,*
and *The Later Roman Empire.**

The Economic Basis
of the Athenian Democracy

Two charges have been brought
against the Athenian democracy, one
both by ancient and by modern critics,
the other in recent times only. The first
is that the pay, which was an essential
part of the system, was provided by the
tribute paid by Athens' allies in the
Delian League, and that the democracy
was therefore parasitic on the empire:
the second, that Athenians only had the
leisure to perform their political functions because they were supported by
slaves—the democracy was in fact parasitic on slavery.

To the first charge there is a very
simple answer, that the democracy continued to function in the fourth century when Athens had lost her empire;
the Second Athenian League, which
lasted effectively only from 377 to 357,
was never a paying proposition, the
contributions of the allies by no means
covering the cost of military and naval
operations. And not only did the democracy continue to function, but a new
and important form of pay, that for
attendance in the assembly, was introduced early in the century. This being
so it is hardly worth while to go into
the financial figures, particularly as there

---

* From A. H. M. Jones, "The Economic Basis of the Athenian Democracy," in *Athenian Democracy* (Oxford, 1957), pp. 5–20. Reprinted by permission of Basil Blackwell, Publisher.

must be many gaps in our calculations. The magistrates numbered about 350 in the later fourth century, and, if they received on an average 1 drachma a day, the annual bill would be 21 talents.[1] The council, if all the members were paid for every day of the year, would have cost rather under 26 talents a year, but if councillors, like jurors, were paid for actual attendance, the bill would be considerably less, since sessions were not held every day and many members did not attend regularly. Assembly pay cannot be calculated as we do not know how large the quorum was. The major item was the 6,000 jurors for whom Aristophanes budgets 150 talents a year, presumably by the simple method of

---

[1] For the convenience of readers unfamiliar with Attic currency, the following table is given:
1 talent=60 minae=6,000 drachmae
   1 mina = 100 drachmae
       1 drachma=6 obols
Owing to the very different standards of living and patterns of spending it is useless and even misleading to try to translate Attic into modern currency, especially now when the value of money is changing so fast. The following facts will give a rough idea of the value of money in fifth- and fourth-century Athens (fourth-century prices and wages were higher than fifth.) In the Erechtheium accounts the standard wage (for citizens, metics and slaves alike) is 1 drachma per day, occasionally 1½ drachmae. In the Eleusinian accounts of 329–328 and 327–326 B.C. unskilled labourers get 1½ drachmae per day, skilled men 2 or 2½ drachmae. In 351 B.C. Demosthenes . . . reckons 2 obols a day as ration allowance for soldiers and sailors: as he is trying to prove that his projected standing force can be cheaply maintained he is probably being optimistic. . . . For the maintenance of two girls and a boy, with a male nurse and a maid, in about 400 B.C. Lysias allows 1,000 drachmae a year and Demosthenes, . . . speaking in 363 B.C., accepts 700 drachmae a year as a reasonable sum for the maintenance of himself and his sister and mother during his minority. These work out at about 3⅓ obols and nearly 4 obols each per day, which seems very little, but rent is not included and Greeks considered that women and children ate much less than men. . . .

multiplying 3 obols by 6,000 jurors by 300 court days (the courts did not sit on the forty or more assembly days nor on the numerous festivals). This is a theoretical maximum, for the whole 6,000 were not empanelled in juries on every court day—Aristophanes' jurors rise at dead of night to queue for their tickets. As against this, the internal revenue of Athens, apart from imperial receipts, can be inferred to have been in the range of 400 talents a year in the fifth century. Since other peace-time expenditure was minimal, pay was thus amply covered by internal income at this period. In the fourth century the revenue dropped considerably; Demosthenes indeed stated that earlier in the century it amounted to only 130 talents. He is perhaps thinking of the regular income from taxes and rents, excluding receipts from fines, confiscations and court fees, which were a considerable proportion of the whole. Even so, we know that in the first half of the fourth century it was at times a tight squeeze. By 340, however, the regular revenue had risen to 400 talents again, and things were easy.

That Athens profited financially from her empire is of course true. But these profits were not necessary to keep the democracy wroking. They enabled Athens to be a great power and to support a much larger citizen population at higher standards of living. One oligarchic critic emphasises the casual profits incidental on Athens' position as an imperial city; the imperial litigation which brought in more court fees, the increased customs revenue, the demand for lodgings, cabs and slaves to hire. Advocates and politicians made money by pleading the legal cases of the allies, and promoting measures in their favour.

But these were chicken-feed compared with the solid benefits of empire, the tribute amounting to 400 talents a year and other imperial income raising the annual total to 600 talents, and the acquisition of land overseas, mainly by confiscation from rebellious allied communities or individuals.

The land was utilised either for colonies, which were technically separate states, but being composed of former Athenian citizens were virtually overseas extensions of the Athenian state, or for cleruchies, that is settlements of Athenians who remained full citizens, liable to Athenian taxation and military service, though in practice they naturally would rarely exercise their citizen rights at Athens. Both types of settlement were normally manned from the poorer citizens. Most will have come from the lowest property class, thetes, who possessed property rated under 2,000 drachmae and were liable only for naval service or as light-armed troops on land. The allotments were (in the one case where figures are given) of sufficient value to qualify the owner to rank as a zeugite, liable to military service as a heavy-armed infantryman or hoplite. By her colonies and cleruchies Athens raised more than 10,000 of her citizens from poverty to modest affluence, and at the same time increased her hoplite force by an even larger number, the cleruchs with their adult sons serving in the ranks of the Athenian army and the colonists as allied contingents.

The tribute was partly spent on the upkeep of a standing navy, partly put to reserve. Pericles is stated to have kept sixty triremes in commission for eight months in the year, and he maintained a fleet of 300 in the dockyards. The dockyards must have given employment to an army of craftsmen, as well as to 500 guards, and the crews of the cruising triremes would have numbered 12,000 men, paid a drachma a day for 240 days in the year. Not all the dockyard workers will have been citizens, nor all the naval ratings, but many thousands of Athenian thetes enjoyed regular well-paid employment thanks to the empire. Of the money put to reserve a part, probably 2,000 talents, was spent on public works, notably the Parthenon and the Propylaea, which again, as Plutarch explains, gave employment to the poorer classes. The remainder formed a war fund of 6,000 talents, which was ultimately spent during the Peloponnesian war on pay to hoplites and sailors.

In response to the favourable economic conditions provided by the empire the population of Athens seems to have risen by leaps and bounds during the half-century between the Persian war (480–479) and the opening of the Peloponnesian war (431). The figures are unfortunately very incomplete and not altogether certain, but the general picture is clear enough; they refer to citizens liable to military and naval service, that is males between 20 and 60. At Salamis (480) the Athenians manned 180 triremes, which required 36,000 men. As Attica had been evacuated and no army was mustered this figure probably represents the whole able-bodied population including resident aliens, so that the citizens may be reckoned at about 30,000. At Artemisium, earlier in the same year, the Athenians, supplemented by the population of the little city of Plataea, had manned 127 triremes (25,400 men, perhaps 20,000 Athenians). As an invasion of Attica was expected the hoplites were probably held in reserve and only thetes served in the fleet.

At Plataea (479) 8,000 Athenian hoplites fought, but a large fleet was simultaneously in commission, which will have carried perhaps 2,000 marines of hoplite status: for Marathon (490) Athens had mustered 9,000 hoplites. These figures suggest a total population of 30,000 citizens, a figure given elsewhere by Herodotus, divided 1 : 2 between hoplites and thetes. At the opening of the Peloponnesian war there were over 20,000 citizen hoplites on the muster rolls. The rise will have been due partly to the general rise in prosperity which enabled many thetes, who owned little or no land, to acquire sufficient house property, slaves or cash capital to qualify as hoplites; but mainly to the grant of allotments of land to thetes in the cleruchies. For the thetic class we have no reliable figures, for the large fleets which Athens commissioned at this period were certainly manned not only by citizens but resident aliens and by foreigners drawn from the cities of the empire. But if, as Plutarch suggests, the sixty ships kept regularly in commission during peace time were largely manned by citizens, the crews of these, together with sundry standing land forces (1,600 archers and 500 shipyard guards, for instance) and the 6,000 jurors, of whom a large proportion were probably thetes, would account for 20,000 men. There were also workers employed in the shipyards, on public works and in private industry, but many of these may have been seasonal, spending the summer rowing and doing other work in the winter. Despite the rise of many thousands into the hoplite class, the thetes must have certainly maintained and probably considerably increased their numbers. Otherwise it would be hard to account for the radical tone of the fifth century democracy, and the predominance, noted with disfavour by oligarchic critics, of the "naval masses" in its councils.

The Peloponnesian war caused great losses both by battle casualties and by the plague: 1,000 hoplites fell at Delium and 600 at Amphipolis, and 2,700 hoplites and 130 triremes carrying perhaps 13,000 citizen sailors, if half the crews were Athenians, were sent to Sicily, of whom only a remnant ever saw Athens again, while in the plague 4,700 men of hoplite status and an uncounted number of thetes perished. Towards the end of the war (411) there seem to have been only 9,000 hoplites resident in Attica, and after the war the cleruchs were all dispossessed. In 322 the hoplite class still numbered only 9,000 despite a revival of prosperity. By that date the thetes numbered only 12,000. Other evidence suggests that both figures were about the same earlier in the century. The loss of the empire and the fall of Athens in 404 must have compelled many thousands of citizens, dispossessed cleruchs and unemployed sailors and dockyard workers, to emigrate or take service as mercenaries abroad. A general decrease in prosperity caused the population to sink to a level well below that of the Persian wars, and in particular reduced the thetic class. Hence the increasingly bourgeois tone of the fourth century democracy.

The second charge against the Athenian democracy, that it was parasitic on slavery, is more difficult to answer with any certainty. It will be as well first to make plain the elements of the problem. The Athenians, like all Greek peoples, regarded themselves as a kinship group, and citizenship depended strictly on descent (always on the father's side and, by a law passed in 451 and reenacted in

403, on the mother's side also) and not on residence, however long. The population of Attica therefore consisted not only of citizens but of free aliens, mainly immigrants who had settled permanently and often lived at Athens for generations, but also including freed slaves and persons of mixed descent; and of slaves, mainly imported but some home-bred. It is unhistorical to condemn the Athenian democracy because it did not give political rights to all residents of Attica; it was the democracy of the Athenian people. It is however relevant to enquire whether the Athenian people was a privileged group depending on the labour of others. Sparta might be called technically a democracy (though the hereditary kings and the council of elders balanced the power of the people) inasmuch as the whole body of Spartiates chose the ephors, in whose hands the government effectively lay, but the Spartiates were a body of rentiers supported by native serfs, the helots, who far outnumbered them. Was the Athenian democracy of this order? The resident aliens (metics) do not concern us here. They made a great contribution to Athenian prosperity, particularly in the fields of industry, commerce and banking—indeed they seem to have dominated the two latter. They were voluntary immigrants and could leave when they wished (except in time of war). That so many domiciled themselves permanently in Attica—a census taken at the end of the fourth century showed 10,000 metics as against 21,000 citizens—is a testimony to their liberal treatment. They enjoyed full civil (as opposed to political) rights, except that they could not own land—hence their concentration on industry and commerce—and were subject to all the duties of citizens,

including military and naval service and taxation at a slightly higher scale. They were a contented class, and many demonstrated their loyalty to their adoptive city by generous gifts at times of crisis.

What of slaves? Here it will be as well to clear up another misconception. It is often stated, mainly on the authority of Plato and Aristotle, that "the Greeks" considered manual work degrading. Now it is true that gentlemen like Plato and Aristotle despised workers and justified their contempt by asserting that manual work deformed the body and the soul. But that this was the attitude of the average poor Greek there is no evidence. An anecdote recorded by Xenophon probably gives a better insight into his point of view. Eutherus, who has lost his overseas estates as a result of the war, has been reduced to earning his living by manual labour. Socrates asks what he will do when his bodily strength fails and suggests that he find a job as a rich man's bailiff. Eutherus is horrified at the suggestion— "I could not endure to be a slave . . . I absolutely refuse to be at any man's beck and call." What the Athenian thete objected to was not hard work— incidentally his main military duty in the fifth century was rowing in the galleys, a task in most later civilisations considered fit only for infidel slaves or convicts—but being another man's servant. He would work as an independent craftsman or at a pinch as a casual labourer, but he would not take even a black-coated job as a regular employee; we find that such highly responsible posts as the manager of a bank or the foreman overseer of a mine are filled by slaves or freedmen of the owner.

Is it true, as we are still too often told, that the average Athenian, in the intervals between listening to a play of Sophocles and serving as a magistrate, councillor or juror, lounged in the market place, discussing politics and philosophy, while slaves toiled to support him? Contemporary critics of the democracy did not think so. Plato's Socrates, analysing the people in a democracy, divides them into the drones, that is the active politicians and their cliques of supporters, and the mass of the people "who support themselves by their labour and do not care about politics, owning very little property; this is the largest and most powerful element in a democracy when it is assembled." Xenophon's Socrates, rebuking Charmides for his shyness at addressing the assembly, asks if he is afraid "of the fullers among them or the shoemakers or the carpenters or the smiths or the peasants or the merchants or the shopkeepers: for the assembly is composed of all of them." Aristotle, analysing the people (that is the mass of poor citizens) in different cities, classifies them as craftsmen, shopkeepers, seamen of various kinds—fishermen, ferrymen, sailors on merchantmen or warships—and casual day labourers and those who have little property so that they can enjoy no leisure. . . .

We have no reliable evidence for the total number of slaves in Attica at any time. For the late fourth century we have two figures, which, if we could rely on them, would be startling. The Byzantine lexicon of Suidas cites Hypereides (probably in connection with his proposal to free the slaves after the battle of Chaeronea in 338 B.C.) as speaking of "more than 150,000 from the silver mines and over the rest of the country." Athenaeus, who wrote at the end of the second century A.D., quotes Ctesicles, a chronicler of unknown date, as stating that at the census held by Demetrius of Phaleron (317–307) 400,000 slaves were registered. These are, as Beloch has convincingly demonstrated, quite impossible figures, and must have been corrupted in the course of their transmission to the late sources in which we read them. To turn to more reliable if less explicit evidence, according to Thucydides more than 20,000 slaves, mainly skilled men, escaped during the ten years' occupation of Deceleia by the Spartans;[2] these would probably be in the main miners and agricultural slaves, but would include many city workers, since the sixteen miles of city walls cannot have been so completely patrolled as to prevent escapes. Xenophon declares that the mines could provide employment for many more than 10,000, as those—if any—who remembered what the slave tax used to fetch before the Deceleian war could testify (he was writing sixty years later). But whatever their numbers their distribution is fairly clear. They were owned in the main by the 1,200 richest families and in decreasing numbers by the next 3,000 or so. It is unlikely that any slaves were owned by two-thirds to three-quarters of the citizen population. The great majority of the citizens earned their living by the work of their hands, as peasant farmers, craftsmen, shopkeepers, seamen and labourers; so contemporary witnesses state, and so the detailed evidence, so far as it goes, suggests. In only one occupation was slave labour predominant, in mining, and even here, contrary to common belief, some citizens worked. Xenophon, advocating that the State

[2] The occupation began in 413 B.C. in northern Attica, not very far from Athens.—*Ed.*

acquire a large body of slaves to be leased to the citizens for use in the mines, suggests that not only will existing contractors add to their manpower but that "there are many of those who are themselves in the mines who are growing old, and many others, both Athenians and aliens, who would not or could not work with their hands, but would gladly make their living by supervising." In one of the Demosthenic speeches we meet a man who boasts "In earlier times I made a lot of money from the silver mines, working and toiling myself with my own hands": he had struck lucky and was now one of the 300 richest men in Athens.

That the poorer citizens lived on State pay for political services is, even for the fourth century, when the system was most fully developed, demonstrably false. A man could only be a councillor two years in his life, and could hold none of the magistracies chosen by lot for more than one annual tenure. He could by attending the assembly—and getting there in time to qualify for pay —earn a drachma on thirty days and 1½ drachmae on ten days in the year. On some festivals—the number varied according to the state of the exchequer— he could draw his theoric payment of 2 obols. On other days, if lucky enough to be successful in the annual ballot for the 6,000 jurors, he could queue in hopes of being empanelled on a jury and earning 3 obols, just enough to feed himself. At this rate a bachelor without dependants could barely with consistent good luck scrape a living; for a man with a family it was quite impossible.

The majority of the citizens were then workers who earned their own livings and whose political pay served only to compensate them in some measure for

loss of working time. Agricultural and industrial slaves in the main merely added to the wealth of a relatively small rentier class, whose principal source of income was land; this same class employed most of the domestic slaves. It only remains to ask how far the Athenian State drew its revenue, directly or indirectly, from slaves. The State owned a certain number of slaves. Most famous are the 1,200 Scythian archers who policed the assembly and the law courts and enforced the orders of the magistrates. There were a number of others ranging from the workers in the mint to the city gaoler and the public slave *par excellence* who had custody of the public records and accounts. Athens thus ran her police force and her rudimentary civil service in part by slave labour —the clerks of the magistrates were mostly salaried citizens. There was apparently a tax on slaves, known only from the mention in Xenophon cited above, but it can hardly have been an important item in the revenue to receive so little notice. The mines, which were mainly exploited by slave labour, also brought in revenue to the State, but less than might have been expected seeing that concessionaires sometimes made large fortunes. The mines flourished in the fifth century, from their first serious exploitation in 483 till the Spartan occupation of Deceleia in 413. They then went through a prolonged bad period till the 330s, when they were again in full swing. We have no figures for the fifth century. In the fourth we have a full record of one year's concessions (367–366), when the sums paid totaled 3,690 drachmae, and a partial record of a later year—probably 342–341 —when the revenue came to about 3 talents. There was probably a royalty payment of one twenty-fourth in addition to the prices paid for concessions. It is somewhat mysterious where the 400 talents of Athenian revenue came from, but a negligible proportion of it arose even indirectly from slave labour.

The charge brought by fifth-century oligarchic critics (and thoughtlessly repeated by many modern writers), that the Athenian democracy depended for its political pay on the tribute of the subject allies, was brought to the test of fact when Athens lost her empire in 404 B.C., and was proved to be a calumny when the democracy continued to pay the citizens for their political functions out of domestic revenues. The modern charge that the Athenian democracy was dependent on slave labour was never brought to the test, since the Athenians never freed all their slaves. This is not surprising, for slavery was an established institution, which most people accepted without question as "according to nature," and to abolish it would have meant a wholesale disregard of the rights of property, which the Athenians throughout their history were careful to respect. It is more surprising that on some occasions of crisis motions for a partial or wholesale freeing of slaves were carried. In 406 all male slaves of military age were freed and granted the citizenship to man the ships which won the battle of Arginusae. After the expulsion of the Thirty in 403, Thrasybulus, the left-wing leader of the restored democracy, carried a measure, later quashed as illegal by the moderate leader Archinus, to free and enfranchise all slaves who had fought for the democracy. In 338, after the defeat of Chaeronea, the left-wing politican Hypereides proposed and carried a motion to free all (able-bodied male) slaves to

resist the Macedonians; this motion was again quashed as illegal by a conservative politican.

These facts suggest that there was no bitterness between the mass of the citizens and the slaves, but rather a sense of fellow-feeling. This was a point which shocked contemporary Athenian oligarchs. The "Old Oligarch" speaks bitterly of the insolence of slaves at Athens, and complains that it is illegal to strike them—the reason, he explains, is that the people are indistinguishable in dress and general appearance from slaves, and it would be easy to strike a citizen by mistake. The moderate oligarch Theramenes is careful to assure his colleagues among the Thirty that he is not one of "those who think there would not be a good democracy until slaves and those who through poverty would sell the city for a drachma participate in it." Plato mocks at the excess of freedom in the democracy, in which "men and women who have been sold are no less free than their purchasers."

Though the Athenians treated their slaves with a humanity which was exceptional according to the standards of the time, they never abolished slavery, and the charge that Athenian democracy was dependent on their labour was never brought to the test of fact. But had Hypereides' motion been allowed to stand, and extended to slaves of all ages and both sexes, it would not seem, on the basis of the evidence cited earlier in this article, that its effects would have been catastrophic. All wealthy and well-to-do citizens (or rather their wives and unmarried daughters) would have been incommoded by having to do their own housework. A very small number of wealthy or comfortably off men who had invested all their money in mining and industrial slaves would have been reduced to penury, and a larger number, but still a small minority, would have lost the proportion of their income which derived from industrial slaves, and would have had to let their farms instead of cultivating them by slave labour. A number of craftsmen would have lost their apprentices and journeymen. But the great majority of Athenians who owned no slaves but cultivated their own little farms or worked on their own as craftsmen, shopkeepers or labourers would have been unaffected.

One of the most far-reaching social changes which took place in Athens in the late fifth and fourth centuries was the growth of individualism. This had its counterpart in economic life in the growth of capitalism. The interplay of these new forces within the political framework of democracy is detailed by J. B. BURY (1861–1927) in his *History of Greece*, which appeared first in 1900 and was subsequently revised by Russell Meiggs, a Fellow of Balliol College, Oxford. Bury was the editor of the first six volumes of the *Cambridge Ancient History*, and wrote many outstanding works, including *The Ancient Greek Historians* and the *History of the Later Roman Empire*, which established him as a Byzantine as well as a classical historian.*

Individualism Versus Equality

When Pericles declared that Athens was the school of Greece, this was rather his ideal of what she should be than a statement of a reality. It would have surprised him to learn that, when imperial Athens fell from her throne, his ideal would be fulfilled. This was what actually happened. It was not until Athens lost her empire that she began to exert a great decisive influence on Greek thought and civilisation. This influence was partly exerted by the establishment of schools in the strict sense—the literary school of Isocrates and the philosophical school of Plato—which attracted to Athens men from all quarters of the Hellenic world. But the increase in the intellectual influence of Athens was largely owing to the fact that she was becoming herself more receptive of influence from without. She was becoming Hellenic as well as Athenian; she was beginning to become even something more than Hellenic. This tendency towards cosmopolitanism had been promoted by philosophical speculation, which rises above national distinctions; and it is manifested variously in the pan-Hellenism of Isocrates, in the attitude of such different men as Plato and Xenophon towards Athens, in the increasing number of foreign religious

* From J. B. Bury, *A History of Greece to the Death of Alexander the Great*, 3d ed., revised by Russell Meiggs (London, 1951), pp. 574–583; 585–588. Reprinted by permission of Macmillan & Co. Ltd., London; St. Martin's Press, Inc.; and The Macmillan Company of Canada, Ltd.

worships established at Athens or Piraeus, in a general decline of local patriotism, and in many other ways. There was perhaps no institution which had a wider influence in educating Greek thought in the fourth century than the theatre; its importance in city life was recognised by practical statesmen. It was therefore a matter of the utmost moment that the old Athenian comedy, turning mainly on local politics, ceased to be written, and a new school of comic poets arose who dealt with subjects of general human interest. Here Athens had a most effectual instrument for spreading ideas. And the tragedies of the fourth century, though as literature they were of less note and consequence than the comedies, were not less significant of the spirit of the time. They were all dominated by the influence of Euripides, the great teacher of rationalism, the daring critic of all established institutions and beliefs. And the comic poets were also under his spell.

It can easily be seen that the cultivation of these wider sympathies was connected with the growth of what is commonly called "individualism." The citizen is no longer content to express his religious feelings simply as one member of the state, and, since his own life has thus become for him something independent of the city, his attitude to the city is transformed. His duty to his country may conflict with his duty to himself as a man; and thus patriotism ceases to be unconditionally the highest virtue. Again, men begin to put to themselves, more or less explicitly, the question whether the state is not made for the individual and not the individual for the state. It followed that greater demands were made upon the state by the citizen for his own private welfare;

and that the citizen, feeling himself tied by no indissoluble bond to his country, was readier than formerly to seek his fortune elsewhere. Thus we find Athenian officers acting independently of their country, in the pay of foreign powers.

A vivid exaggerated description of this spirit has been drawn by Plato in one of his famous contributions to political science, the *Republic.* "The horses and asses," he says, "have a way of marching along with all the rights and dignities of freemen; and they will run at anybody whom they meet in the street if he does not leave the road clear for them: and all things are just ready to burst with liberty." When he describes the excessive freedom of democracy, he is dealing with the growth of individualism, as a result of freedom in its constitutional sense; but his argument that individualism is the fatal fruit of a democratic constitution rests largely on the double sense of the word "freedom." The notable thing is that no man did more to promote the tendencies which are here deplored by Plato than Plato himself and his fellow philosophers. If any single man could be held responsible for the inevitable growth of individualism, it would be perhaps Euripides; but assuredly, next to Euripides, it would be Plato's revered master, Socrates, the son of Sophroniscus.

When the history of Greece was being directed by Pericles and Cleon, Nicias and Lysander, men little dreamed either at Athens or elsewhere that the interests of the world were far more deeply concerned in the doings of one eccentric Athenian who held aloof from public affairs. The ideas which we owe to Socrates are now so organically a part of the mind of civilised men that it is hard to appreciate the intellectual power which was required to originate them. Socrates was the first champion of the supremacy of the intellect as a court from which there is no appeal; he was the first to insist that a man must order his life by the guidance of his own intellect. Socrates was thus a rebel against authority as such; and he shrank from no consequences. He did not hesitate to show his companions that an old man has no title to respect because he is old, unless he is also wise; or that an ignorant parent has no claim to obedience on the mere account of the parental relation. Knowledge and veracity, the absolute sovereignty of the understanding, regardless of consequences, regardless of all prejudices connected with family or city—this was the ideal of Socrates, consistently and uncompromisingly followed.

But men using their intellects often come to different conclusions. The command issued by an authority which Socrates may reject has been, directly or ultimately, the result of some mental process. It is manifest that we require a standard of truth and an explanation of the causes of error. The solution of Socrates is, briefly, this. When we make a judgment, we compare two ideas; and in order to do so correctly it is obvious that these ideas must be clear and distinct; error arises from comparing ideas that are undefined and vague. Definition was thus the essential point—and it was an essential novelty—in the Socratic method for arriving at truth. Its necessity is a commonplace now; and we have rather to guard against its dangers.

The application of this method to ethics was the chief occupation of Socrates, for the interests of human life and its perplexities entirely absorbed him. In the history of ethics his position is supreme; he was the founder of utilitarianism. He arrived at the doctrine by analysing the notion of "good"; the result of his analysis was that "the good is the useful." Closely connected was the principle that virtue is happiness, and this was the basis of the famous Socratic paradox that no man willingly does wrong, but only through ignorance, for there is no man who would not will his own happiness. It is easy to point out the errors of this startling statement; it is perhaps easier to forget how much wrong-doing is due to the confused thinking of clouded brains and the ignorance of untrained minds.

The man who had no respect for authority was not likely to except the gods from the range of his criticism; and the popular religion could not sustain examination. Socrates was as little orthodox as Anaxagoras and other "impious" philosophers; but he made no new departure in the field of theology. He doubtless believed in the existence of a God; but as to the nature of the divine principle he was probably what we call an "agnostic," as he certainly was in regard to the immortality of the soul.

Socrates then was the originator of a new logical method, the founder of utilitarianism, and, above all, the unsparing critic of all things in heaven and earth—or rather on earth only, for he disdained things in heaven as uninteresting and irrelevant,—a fearless critic, undeterred by any feeling of piety or prejudice. He never wrote anything, he only conversed. But he conversed with the ablest young men of the day who were destined afterwards to become immortal themselves as thinkers; he communicated to them—to Plato, to Aristippus, to Euclides—his own spirit of scepticism and criticism; he imbued them with intellectual courage and intellectual freedom. He never preached, he only discussed; that was the Socratic method—dialectic or the conversational method. He did not teach, for he professed to have no knowledge; he would only confess that he was exceptional in knowing that he knew nothing: this was the Socratic irony. He went about showing that most popular notions, as soon as they are tested, prove to be inconsistent and untenable; he wished to convince every man he met that his convictions would not stand examination. We can easily conceive how stimulating this was to the young men, and how extremely irritating to the old. Haunting the market-places and the gymnasia Socrates was always ready to entrap men of all ages and ranks into argument, and many a grudge was owed him by reverend and conceited seniors, whose foggy minds he exposed to ridicule by means of his prudent interrogations. Though no man ever taught more effectually than Socrates, he was not a teacher, he had no course of lectures to give, and therefore he took no fee. Herein lay his distinction from the sophists, to whom by his speculation, his scepticism, his mastery of argument, his influence over young men, he naturally belongs, and with whom he was generally classed. He soon became a notorious figure in the streets of Athens; nature had marked him out among other men by his grotesque satyr-like face.

Though he was the child of democracy, born to a heritage of freedom in a city where the right of free discussion was unrestrained, the sacred name of democracy was not more sheltered than anything else from the criticism of Socrates. He railed, for instance, at the system of choosing magistrates by lot, one of the protections of democracy at Athens. He was unpopular with the mass, for he was an enemy of shams and ignorance and superstition. Honest democrats of the type of Thrasybulus and Anytus, who did their duty but had no desire to probe its foundations, regarded him as a dangerous freethinker who spent his life in diffusing ideas subversive of the social order. They might point to the ablest of the young men who had kept company with him, and say: "Behold the fruits of his conversation! Look at Alcibiades, his favourite companion, who has done more than any other man to ruin his country. Look at Critias, who, next to Alcibiades, has wrought the deepest harm to Athens; who, brought up in the Socratic circle, first wrote a book against democracy, then visited Thessaly and stirred up the serfs against their masters, and finally, returning here, inaugurated the reign of terror. Look, on the other hand, at Plato, an able young man, whom the taste for idle speculation, infused by Socrates, has seduced from the service of his country. Or look at Xenophon, who, instead of serving Athens, has gone to serve her enemies. Truly Socrates and his propaganda have done little good to the Athenian state." However unjust any particular instance might seem, it is easy to understand how considerations of this kind would lead many practical unspeculative men to look upon Socrates and his ways with little favour. And from their point of view, they were perfectly right. His spirit, and the ideas that he made current, were an insidious menace to the cohesion of the social fabric, in which there was not a stone or a joint that he did not question. In other words, he was the active apostle of individualism, which led in its further development to the subversion of that local patriotism which had inspired the cities of Greece in her days of greatness.

And this thinker, whose talk was shaking the Greek world in its foundations, though none guessed it, was singled out by the Delphic priesthood for a distinguished mark of approbation. In the truest oracle that was ever uttered from the Pythian tripod, it was declared that no one in the world was wiser than Socrates. We know not at what period of the philosopher's career this answer was given, but, if it was seriously meant, it showed a strange insight which we should hardly have looked for at the shrine of Delphi. The motive of the oracle concerning the wisdom of Socrates is an unsolved problem. If it were an attempt to enlist his support, in days when religion was threatened by such men as Anaxagoras, it shows an unexpected perception of his importance, united with a by no means surprising blindness to the significance of his work.

Socrates died five years after the fall of the Athenian empire, and the manner of his death set a seal upon his life. It was thought that the philosopher, who had been the friend of Critias, was a danger to the democracy, and should be removed; but the political motive was kept in the background. Anytus, the honest democratic politician who had been prominent in the restoration of the democracy, came forward, with some others, as a champion of the state religion, and accused Socrates of impiety. The accusation ran: "Socrates is guilty of crime, because he does not believe in the gods recognised by the city, but introduces strange supernatural beings; he is also guilty, because he corrupts the youth." The penalty proposed was death; but the accusers had no desire to inflict it; they expected that, when the charge was lodged in the archon's office, Socrates would leave Attica, and no one would have hindered him from doing so. But Socrates was full of days—he had reached the age of seventy—and life spent otherwise than in conversing in the streets of Athens would have been worthless to him. He surprised the city by remaining to answer the charge. The trial was heard in a court of 501 judges, the king-archon presiding, and the old philosopher was found guilty by a majority of sixty. It was a small majority, considering that the general truth of the accusation was undeniable. According to the practice of Athenian law, it was open to a defendant when he was condemned to propose a lighter punishment than that fixed by the accuser, and the judges were required to choose one of the two sentences. Socrates might have saved his life if he had proposed an adequate penalty, but he offered only a small fine, and was consequently condemned, by a much larger majority, to death. He drank the cup of doom a month later, discoursing with his disciples as eagerly as ever till his last hour. "I am persuaded that it was better for me to die now, and to be released from trouble."

The actual reply of Socrates at his trial has not been preserved, but we know its tone and spirit and much of its tenor. For it supplied his companion Plato, who was present, with the material of a work which stands absolutely alone in literature. In the *Apology of Socrates*, Plato has succeeded in catching the personality of the master and conveying its stimulus to his readers.

There can be no question that this work reproduces the general outline of the actual defence, which is here wrought into an artistic form. And we see how utterly impossible it was for Socrates to answer the accusation. He enters into an explanation of his life and motives, and has no difficulty in showing that many things popularly alleged against him are false. But with the actual charge of holding and diffusing heterodox views he deals briefly and unsatisfactorily. He was not condemned unjustly—according to the law. And that is the intensity of the tragedy. There have been no better men than Socrates; and yet his accusers were perfectly right. It is not clear why their manifesto for orthodoxy was made at that particular time; but it is probable that twenty years later such an action would have been a failure. Perhaps the facts of the trial justify us in the rough conclusion that two out of every five Athenian citizens then were religiously indifferent. In any case the event had a wider than a merely religious significance. The execution of Socrates was the protest of the spirit of the old order against the growth of individualism.

Seldom in the course of history have violent blows of this kind failed to recoil upon the striker and serve the cause they were meant to harm. Socrates was remembered at Athens with pride and regret. His spirit began to exercise an influence which the tragedy of his death enhanced. His companions never forgave the democracy for putting their master to death; he lived and grew in the study of their imaginations; and they spent their lives in carrying on his work.

They carried forward his work, but they knew not what they were doing. They had no suspicion that in pursuing those speculations to which they were stimulated by the Socratic method they were sapping the roots of Greek city life as it was known to the men who fought at Marathon. Plato was a true child of Socrates, and yet he was vehement in condemning that individualism which it had been the lifework of Socrates to foster. Few sights are stranger than Plato and Xenophon turning their eyes away from their own free country to regard with admiration the constitution of Sparta, where their beloved master would not have been suffered so much as to open his mouth. It was a distinct triumph for the Lacedaemonians when their constitution, which the Athenians of the age of Pericles regarded as old-fashioned machinery, was selected by the greatest thinker of Athens as the nearest existing approach to the ideal. Indeed the Spartan organisation, at the very time when Sparta was making herself detested throughout Greece, seems to have attracted general admiration from political thinkers. It attracted them because the old order survived there,—the citizen absolutely submissive to the authority of the state, and not looking beyond it. Elsewhere they were troubled by the problem of reconciling the authority of the state with the liberty of the individual citizen; at Sparta there was no such trouble, for the state was absolute. Accordingly they saw in Sparta the image of what a state should be; just because it was relatively free from that individualism which they were themselves actively promoting by their speculations in political philosophy. How freely such speculations ranged at this time is illustrated by the fact that the fundamental institution of ancient society, slavery, was called in question. It had indeed been called in question by Euripides, and the hetero-dox "modern" views of Euripides were coming into fashion. One thinker expounded the doctrine that slavery was unnatural. Speculation even went so far as to stir the question of the political subjection of women. The *Parliament of Women*, a comedy of Aristophanes, ridicules women's rights; and in Plato's ideal *Republic* women are on a political equality with men. Socialistic theories were also rife, and were a mark for the mockery of Aristophanes in the same play. Plato seized upon the notion of communism and made it one of the principles of his ideal state. But his object was not that of the ordinary "collectivist," to promote the material well-being of all; but rather to make his citizens better, by defending them against poverty and ambition. Before he died, Plato had come to the conviction that communism was impracticable, and in the state which he adumbrated in his old age he recognised private property —though he vested the ownership not in the individual but in the family.

In this period—during the fifty years after the battle of Aegospotami—the art of writing prose was brought to perfection at Athens; and this is closely connected with the characteristic tendency which has engaged our attention. While Socrates and others had been bringing about a revolution in thought, the Sicilian Gorgias and other professors of rhetoric or style had been preparing an efficient vehicle for diffusing ideas. Prose is the natural instrument of criticism and argument; it is a necessary weapon for intellectual persuasion; and therefore the fourth century is an age of prose. The circumstance that the great Athenian poets of the fifth century had no successors in the fourth does not

prove any decline in brains or in imagination. If Plato had been born half a century earlier he would have been a rival of Aeschylus and Sophocles. If Aeschylus and Sophocles had been born two or three generations later they would have expressed their genius in prose. Euripides, who has come under the influence of the critical spirit, seems sometimes like a man belated; he uses the old vehicle to convey thoughts for which it was hardly suited. It must always be remembered that the great dramatic poems of the fifth century bore an inalienable religious character; and, as soon as the day came when the men of the highest literary faculty were no longer in touch with the received religion, drama of the old kind ceased to be written. That is why the fourth century is an age of prose; tragic poetry owes its death to Euripides and the Socratic spirit. The eager individualism of the age found its natural expression in prose, whose rhythmical periods demanded almost as much care and art as poetry; and the plastic nature of the Greek language rendered it a most facile instrument for the purposes of free thought and criticism.

Thus Athens became really a school for Greece, as soon as that individualism prevailed which Pericles had unwittingly foreshadowed in the very same breath: "I say that Athens is the school of Hellas, and that the individual Athenian in his own person seems to have the power of adapting himself to the most varied forms of action with the utmost versatility and grace."

The form and features of an age are wont to be mirrored in its art; and one effective means of winning a concrete notion of the spirit of the fourth century is to study the works of Praxiteles and compare them with the sculptures which issued from the workshop of Phidias. Just as the citizen was beginning to assert his own individuality as more than a mere item in the state, so the plastic artist was emancipating his art from its intimate connexion with the temples of the gods, and its subordination to architecture. For in the fifth century, apart from a few colossal statues like those which Phidias wrought for Athens and Olympia, the finest works of the sculptor's chisel were to decorate frieze or pediment. In the fourth century the architect indeed still required the sculptor's service; Scopas, for instance, was called upon in his youth to decorate the temple of Athena Alea at Tegea, in his later years to make a frieze for the tomb of a Carian prince; but, in general, the sculptor developed his art more independently of architecture, and all the great works of Praxiteles were complete in themselves and independent. And, as sculpture was emancipating itself from the old subordination to architecture, so it also emancipated itself from the religious ideal. In the age of Phidias, the artist who fashioned a god sought to express in human shape the majesty and immutability of a divine being; and this ideal had been perfectly achieved. In the fourth century the deities lose their majesty and changelessness; they are conceived as physically perfect men and women, with human feelings though without human sorrows; they are invested with human personalities. The contrast may be seen by looking at the group of gods in the frieze of the Parthenon, and then at some of the works of Praxiteles: the Hermes, which was set up in the temple of Hera at Olympia, and is preserved

there; the Aphrodite of Cnidus—a woman shrinking from revealing her beauty as she enters the bath; or the Satyr, with the shape of a man and the mind of a beast. Thus sculpture is marked by "individualism" in a double sense. Each artist is freer to work out an individual path of his own; and the tendency of all artists is to portray the individual man or woman rather than the type, and even the individual phase of emotion rather than the character.

The general spirit of the Athenians in their political life corresponds to this change. Men came more and more to regard the state as a means for administering to the needs of the individual. We might almost say that they conceived it as a co-operative society for making profits to be divided among the members; this at least was the tendency of public opinion. They were consequently more disinclined to enter upon foreign undertakings which were not either necessary for the protection and promotion of their commerce or likely to fill their purses. The fourth century was therefore for Athens an age of less ambition and glory, but of greater happiness and freedom, than the fifth.

The decisive circumstance for Athens was that, while she lost her empire, she did not lose her commerce. This was a cruel blow to Corinth, since it was to destroy Athenian trade that Corinth had brought about the war. The fact shows on how firm foundations Athenian commerce rested. The only rival Athens had to fear was Rhodes, which was becoming a centre of traffic in the south-eastern Mediterranean, but was not destined to interfere seriously with Athenian trade for a long time yet. The population of Attica had declined; plague and war reduced the number of adult male citizens from at least 40,000 to some 22,000. But that was not unfortunate, for there were no longer outsettlements to receive the surplus of the population; and even with the diminished numbers there was a surplus which sought employment in foreign mercenary service. The mercantile development of Athens is shown by the increase of the Piraeus at the expense of the city, in which many plots of ground now became deserted, and by the growth of private banks. It had long been a practice to deposit money in temples, and the priesthoods used to lend money on interest. This suggested to money-changers the idea of doing likewise; and Pasion[1] founded a famous house at Athens, which operated with a capital of fifty talents, and had credit at all Greek centres of commerce. Thus business could be transacted by exchanging letters of credit instead of paying in coin; and the introduction of this system, even on such a small scale, shows the growth of mercantile activity. Money was now much more plentiful, and prices far higher, than before. This was due to the large amount of the precious metals, chiefly gold, which had been brought into circulation in the Greek world in the last quarter of the fifth century. The continuous war led to the coining of the treasures which had been accumulating for many years in temples; and the banking system circulated the money which would otherwise have been hoarded in private houses. But, although the precious metals became plentiful, the rate of interest did not fall; men could still get 12 percent for a loan of their money. This fact is highly significant; it shows clearly that industries were more thriving and trade more active, and consequently capital in greater demand. The high rate of interest must always be remembered when we read of a Greek described as wealthy with a capital which would nowadays seem small.

Communistic ideas were a consequence, perhaps inevitable, of the growth of individualism and the growth of capital. The poorer burghers became more and more acutely alive to the inconsistency between the political equality of all citizens and the social and economical advantages enjoyed by the rich. Political equality seemed to point to social equality as its logical sequel; in fact, full and equal political equality could not be secured without social equality also, since the advantages of wealth necessarily involve superiorities in political influence. Thus, just as in modern Europe, so in ancient Greece, capital and democracy produced socialists, who pleaded for a levelling of classes by means of a distribution of property by the state. Aristophanes mocked these speculations in his *Parliament of Women* and his *Wealth*. The idea of communism which Plato develops on lines of his own in the *Republic* was not an original notion of the philosopher's brain, but was suggested by the current communistic theories of the day. It is well worthy of consideration that the Athenians did not take the step from political to social democracy; and this discretion may have been partly due to the policy of those statesmen who, doubtless conscious of the danger, regarded the theoric fund as an indispensable institution.

The changed attitude of the individual to the state is shown by the

---

[1] Pasion was a freedman who began virtually penniless and built one of the great banking fortunes in the fourth century.—*Ed.*

introduction of a fixed remuneration of half a drachma to Athenian citizens for attending the meetings of the Assembly; and the rise in prices is illustrated by the subsequent increase of this remuneration. For the regular sessions, in which the proceedings were unattractive, the pay was raised to a drachma and a half; for the other meetings, which were more exciting, it was fixed at a drachma. The remuneration for serving in the law-courts was not increased; it was found that half a drachma was sufficient to draw applicants for the judge's ticket. Payment for the discharge of political duties was part of the necessary machinery of the democracy, but the distribution of "spectacle-money" to the poor citizens was a luxury which involved an entirely different principle. It is uncertain when the practice of giving the price of his theatre ticket to the poor Athenian was first introduced; it has been attributed to Pericles, but it is possible that it was not introduced till Athens began to recover after the fall of her empire. In any case, the principle became established in the fourth century of distributing "theoric" moneys, which were supposed to be spent on religious festivals; the citizens came to look forward to frequent and large distributions; the surplus revenue of the state, instead of being saved for emergencies, was placed in the theoric fund; and this theoric fund became so important that it ultimately required a special minister of finance to manage it. Those statesmen under whose guidance the theoric doles were most liberal had naturally the greatest influence with the mass of the citizens; and consequently finance acquired a new importance, and financial ability was developed in a very high degree. The state thus assumed the character of a commercial society; dividends were a political necessity, and in order to meet it heavier taxation was demanded. We have seen how, when war broke out with Sparta, in the year in which the Second Athenian Confederacy was formed, a property-tax was imposed, and the properties of the citizens were assessed anew for this purpose.

Thus the state provided for the comfort of its poorer burghers at the expense of their wealthier fellows. It is, as it were, publicly recognised as a principle of political science that the end of the state is the comfort and pleasure of its individual members; and everything has to be made subordinate to this principle which is outwardly embodied in the theoric fund.

The *Constitution of the Athenians*, part of which is reprinted here, is a tract or pamphlet by an unknown opponent of Athenian democracy. It was once, but is no longer, ascribed to Xenophon; the author, who probably wrote in the last quarter of the fifth century, is now referred to as the OLD OLIGARCH. His prejudice is self-evident, but his information is reliable. His point of view has provided grist for the mills of many historians since his most trenchant criticism is that Athenian democracy was, in reality, the rule of one class, even the tyranny of one class—a specific case, perhaps, of the dictum that "democrats may win, but democracy never."*

▶ *The Tyranny of the Many*

Now, as concerning the Polity of the Athenians, and the type or manner of constitution which they have chosen, I praise it not, in so far as the very choice involves the welfare of the baser folk as opposed to that of the better class. I repeat, I withhold my praise so far; but, given the fact that this is the type agreed upon, I propose to show that they set about its preservation in the right way; and that those other transactions in connection with it, which are looked upon as blunders by the rest of the Hellenic world, are the reverse.

In the first place, I maintain, it is only just that the poorer classes and the People of Athens should have the advantage over the men of birth and wealth, seeing that it is the people who row the vessels, and put round the city her girdle of power. For the steersman, the boatswain, the commanders of fifty, the lookout-man at the prow, the shipwright—these are the people who engird the city with power far rather than her heavy infantry and men of birth and quality. This being the case, it seems only just that offices of state should be thrown open to every one both by the lot and by the show of hands, and that the right of speech should belong to any citizen who likes, without restriction. Further, there are many of these offices which, according as they are in good

* From *The Constitution* [*Polity*] *of the Athenians*, translated by H. G. Dakyns, revised by E. G. Sihler, in *Hellenic Civilization* (Records of Civilization: Sources and Studies) [New York, 1920], pp. 222–225; 231–232. Reprinted by permission of the Columbia University Press.

or in bad hands, are a source of safety or of danger to the People and in these the People prudently abstain from sharing; as, for instance, they do not think it incumbent on themselves to share in the drawing of lots for general or commander of cavalry. The sovereign People recognize the fact that in foregoing the personal exercise of these offices and leaving them to the control of the more competent citizens, they secure the balance of advantage to themselves. It is only those departments of government which bring emolument and assist the private households that the People care to keep in their own hands.

In the next place, in regard to what some people are puzzled to explain—the fact that everywhere greater consideration is shown to the base, to poor people and to common folk, than to persons of good quality,—so far from being a matter of surprise, this, as can be shown, is the keystone of the preservation of the democracy. It is these poor people, this common folk, this riff-raff, whose prosperity, combined with the growth of their numbers, enhance the democracy. Whereas a shifting of fortune to the advantage of the wealthy and the better classes implies the establishment on the part of the commonalty of a strong power in opposition to itself. In fact, all the world over the cream of society is in opposition to the democracy. Naturally, since the smallest amount of intemperance and injustice, together with the highest scrupulousness in the pursuit of excellence, is to be found in the ranks of the better class, while within the ranks of the People will be found the greatest amount of ignorance, disorderliness and rascality,—poverty acting as a strong incentive to base conduct, not to speak of lack of education and ignorance, traceable to the want of means

which afflicts some portions of mankind.

The objection may be raised that it was a mistake to allow the universal right of speech and a seat in council. These privileges should have been reserved for the cleverest, the flower of the community. But here again it will be found that they are acting with wise deliberation in granting to even the baser sort the right of speech, for supposing only the better people might speak, or sit in council, blessings would fall to the lot of those like themselves, but to the commonalty the reverse of blessings. Whereas now, any one who likes, any base fellow, may get up and discover something to the advantage of himself and his equals. It may be retorted: "And what sort of advantage either for himself or for the People can such a fellow be expected to discern?" The answer is, that in their judgment the ignorance and the baseness of this fellow, together with his good will, are worth a great deal more to them than your superior person's virtue and wisdom, coupled with aversion. What it comes to, therefore, is that a state founded upon such institutions will not be the best state; but, given a democracy, these are the right means to secure its preservation. The People, it must be borne in mind, do not demand that the city should be well governed and themselves slaves. They desire to be free and to be masters. As to bad legislation, they do not concern themselves about that. In fact, what you believe to be poor legislation is the very source of the People's strength and freedom. But if you seek for good laws, in the first place you will see the cleverest members of the community laying down the laws for the rest. And in the next place, the better class will curb and chastise the lower orders; the better class will deliberate in behalf of the state, and not suffer men in fits of madness to sit in council, or to speak or vote in the assembly. No doubt; but under the weight of such blessings the People would in a very short time be reduced to slavery.

Further, states oligarchically governed are forced to ratify their alliances and solemn oaths in a substantial fashion, and if they fail to abide by their treaties, the offence, by whomsoever committed, lies nominally at the door of the oligarchs who entered upon the contract. But in the case of engagements entered into by a democracy it is open to the People to throw the blame on the single individual who spoke in favor of some measure, or who put it to the vote, and to enter a denial for the rest of the citizens, averring that one was not present, or did not approve of the terms of the agreement. Inquiries are made in a full meeting of the People, and should any of these things be disapproved of, the demus has devised already innumerable excuses to avoid doing whatever they do not wish. If too any mischief should spring out of any deliberations of the assembly, the People charge that a handful of men acting against the interests of the citizens have ruined the state. But if any good result ensue, they, the People, at once take the credit of that to themselves.

In the same spirit it is not allowed to caricature on the comic stage or otherwise libel the People, because they do not care to hear themselves ill spoken of. But if any one has a desire to satirize his neighbor, he has full leave to do so. And this because they are well aware that, as a general rule, the person caricatured does not belong to the People, or the masses. He is more likely to be some

wealthy or well-born person, or man of means and influence. In fact, but few poor people and of the popular stamp incur the comic lash, or if they do, they have brought it on themselves by excessive love of meddling or some covetous self-seeking at the expense of the People, so that no particular annoyance is felt at seeing such folk satirized.

What I venture to assert is therefore that the People of Athens have no difficulty in recognizing which of their citizens are of the better sort and which the opposite. Recognizing, accordingly, those who are serviceable and advantageous to themselves, even though they be base, the People love them; but the good folk they are disposed the rather to hate. This excellence of theirs, the People hold, is not ingrained in their nature for any good to itself, but rather for its injury. In direct opposition to this, there are some persons who, being born of the People, are yet by natural instinct not commoners. For my part I pardon the People their democracy, as indeed it is pardonable in any one to do good to himself. But the man who, not being himself one of the People, prefers to live in a state democratically governed rather than in an oligarchical state takes steps to commit wrong. He knows that a bad man has a better chance of slipping through the fingers of justice in a democratic than in an oligarchical state.

I repeat that my position concerning the polity of the Athenians is this: the type of polity is not to my taste, but given that a democratic form of government has been agreed upon, they do seem to me to go the right way to preserve the democracy by the adoption of the particular type which I have set forth.

Part of the value of this article by FRANK W.
WALBANK (1909–   ) is that he places the
decline of Athenian democracy in the context of the
over-all decline of classical civilization: he makes
the point that the decline, so evident in the
Hellenistic era, had its roots in the classical city-state.
Why, he asks, was the theory of democracy arrested?
And to whose interest was it to limit the practice
of democracy? Walbank, Rathbone Professor of
Ancient History and Classical Archaeology at the
University of Liverpool, has contributed to the
Cambridge Economic History of Europe, vol. II, and
to several volumes of *The Year's Work in Classical
Studies*. His book *The Decline of the Roman Empire
in the West* is an analysis of the larger problem.*

Political Equality:
An Arrested Development

In one of the most popular anthology passages in Latin, Servius Sulpicius, writing to console Cicero for his daughter's death, describes how, as he reached Greek waters, sailing from Asia, he began to look about him at the ruins of Greece. "Behind me was Aegina, in front of me Megara, on the right the Piraeus, on the left Corinth, cities which had once been prosperous, but now lay shattered ruins before my sight." *Oppidum cadavera* he goes on to call them —corpses of cities! The picture, it will probably be objected, is overdrawn; certainly the ruin of Greece was, by Cicero's time, already a rhetorical commonplace, to be echoed by Horace, Ovid and Seneca in turn. But it was based upon an essential truth. The Saronic Gulf, once the centre of the world, was now, for all that Greece meant, a dead lake lapping about the foundations of dead cities. In that tragic decay—which was not confined to mainland Greece— we are confronted with one of the most urgent problems of ancient history, and one with a special significance for our generation, who were already living in an age of economic, political and spiritual upheaval, even before the bombs began to turn our own cities into shattered ruins.

* From F. W. Walbank, "The Causes of Greek Decline," *Journal of Hellenic Studies*, vol. 64 (1944), pp. 10–20. Reprinted with the permission of the author and the Society for the Promotion of Hellenic Studies.

This, then, is my reason for reopening a subject on which there is scope for such diverse opinion. . . . If any further justification is required, then I will only add that the recent publication of Prof. Michael Rostovtzeff's classic study of the social and economic life of the Hellenistic Age is at once an invitation and a challenge.[1]

With this work Rostovtzeff completes an historical survey reaching from Alexander to Constantine;[2] and, throughout, he lays stress very emphatically upon the word "history." His four volumes are designed not simply as a compilation of factual material, but as an interpretation of the historical development of six hundred years of ancient civilisation. Both histories, the Hellenistic and the Roman, are pessimistic in outlook, for both recount a failure; in the one case that of Greek and Hellenistic civilisation, in the other the collapse of the ancient world itself. Yet there is a difference of tone. In 1926 the author had ended on a now famous query. "Is it possible," he asked, "to extend a higher civilisation to the lower classes without debasing its standard and diluting its quality to the vanishing point? Is not every civilisation bound to decay as soon as it penetrates the mass?" These questions, with their echoes of Plato, go far beyond the scope of the particular problem of the decay of classical culture, and were undoubtedly prompted by the writer's own personal experience as an *émigré* from Soviet Russia. And in the formulation of certain other problems —Why was the victorious advance of

capitalism stopped? Why was machinery not invented? Why were the business systems not perfected? Why were the primal forces of primitive economy not overcome?—and especially in his interpretation of the chaos of the third century A.D. as a proletarian revolution carried out through the army, his view of ancient history appears to have been influenced by his own vivid apprehension of certain contemporary events in Europe. The comparison between Bolshevik Russia and the ancient world in decay is constantly implicit in his narrative, and frequently he pauses to draw a direct analogy.

Many of these questions are fundamental to the problem of the collapse of ancient civilisation; yet, having raised them, Rostovtzeff left them unanswered. Meanwhile his links with Russia were broken, and in any case events took a turn which falsified his earlier comparison; and so, for a variety of reasons, when in 1941 he published his study of the earlier period, he apparently no longer felt it so urgent a matter even to ask these questions, though, as Prof. Gordon Childe points out, they are equally pertinent to the problem of why Greece and the Hellenistic World went so far and no farther. For in fact the Greek and the Roman failures are in essence one. No one can read through Rostovtzeff's work without being struck by the way in which the earlier forms of decay foreshadow the later, and how, *mutatis mutandis*, the end of Augustus's empire is in its general features an echo of the end of Alexander's. Both failures, in fact, sprang from something deep in the very character of classical civilisation.

The problem of Greek decline may be approached from two sides. First, in the

[1] M. Rostovtzeff, *A Social and Economic History of the Hellenistic World*, Oxford, 1941.

[2] The earlier volume is, of course, Rostovtzeff's *Social and Economic History of the Roman Empire*, (Oxford, 1926).—*Ed.*

social-political sphere there is the failure of the Greeks to achieve the unity which alone might have enabled them to preserve their freedom from outside conquest. In this respect the conflicts between Alexander's successors are a repetition on a larger scale of the old wars of the city-states; there was the same fatal disunity, the same squandering of material and cultural capital, the same ultimate betrayal to the outside enemy.

This failure was one of which many Greeks were themselves conscious. Persia, Macedon and Rome are three stages in a tragic descent, three notes which find a constant echo in the propaganda and ideology of the third and second centuries B.C. . . .

Secondly, there is the cultural failure of the Hellenistic age. At an early date the Greek intellect had gained unrivalled success in its clarity and breadth of thought. The observational science of the Ionians (albeit still wedded to the remnants of pre-rational thinking), the splendid objectivity of Thucydides, the unity of theory and practice in the works of the Hippocratic school, had all pointed forward to further intellectual triumphs; while in the Attic tragedians the moral problems of man's relations with the forces inside himself and inside society had been cast into an artistic form which made its direct appeal to the whole population of Athens. Yet the dawn was false. At the highest moment of the Athenian achievement, in Plato himself, notwithstanding his many magnificent contributions to human thought, the gates were opened to the enemy. The *Laws*, Plato's last attempt to construct the just city, is concerned with the implanting of beliefs and attitudes convenient to authority through the medium of suggestion, and not with the stimulation of man's native curiosity to seek and enquire. A strict and ruthless censorship, the substitution of myths and emotional ceremonies for factual knowledge, the isolation of the citizen from contact with the outside world, the creation of types with standardised reactions, the invoking of the sanctions of a police-state against all kinds of nonconformity—this is Plato's final disastrous contribution to Greek political thought.

Even so, it is as much a sympton as a cause. It represents Plato's reaction to the catastrophe of Aegospotami and to his personal experience of democracy, as he saw it in action at Athens and Syracuse. And though the day was passing when the separate city-state could still be the vehicle of man's intellectual and political progress, he closed his eyes to history and sacrificed the substance of Greek achievement to preserve the husk. In this he was not alone. Aristotle too, for all his mastery in the sphere of scientific observational method, remained politically identified with an obsolescent environment. His *Politics* pre-suppose the city-state throughout. . . . In all the Hellenistic philosophies, likewise, though their field of contemplation had expanded beyond the walls of the city, there is nevertheless a common note of defeat, a drawing-in of the scope of human thought and endeavour. To the disintegration of society the Cynic reply was to "deface the currency," a sharp criticism of all ideals and all standards, the indulging of moral indignation, in short no constructive answer at all. The Stoics turned their thoughts inwards, and sought to proof the individual soul against the raging storms of Fortune; and the Epicureans, though drawing on the materialist speculations of Democritus, also laid their emphasis on the separate moral problem, and tried to live unnoticed in their Garden.

No one, examining the evidence of Greek failure, cultural and social-political, can fail to perceive how closely the two aspects are interwoven. Yet neither is the cause of the other: both reflect something deeper and more fundamental, something which had begun to operate before the end of the fifth century. For the decline of the Greek world, though worked out to its bitter end under the Hellenistic kings and leagues, goes back to cultures already active within the body of the city-state. This more fundamental cause is rooted in the social relation of the classes. It reveals itself most clearly in the failure of the middle class inside the Greek cities to maintain and extend democracy.

At Athens, of which we know most, the rise of the middle class followed the revolutionary changes of the sixth century, when the aristocracy finally capitulated before the successive blows of Solon, Peisistratus and Cleisthenes. The fruit of this victory was Athenian democracy and the defeat of the Persian armada. But success brought new ambitions and new opportunities; and very soon the Athenian fleet, the democratic instrument of Salamis, was being employed as the police force of the Athenian empire. Democracy had become imperialism, forms of society ultimately inconsistent. And though the Athenian defeat at Aegospotami meant the end of the empire, the vice of exclusiveness persisted. The democrats fought with courage and idealism to suppress the oligarchy of Plato's friend Critias, and the rest of the Thirty; but it was the restored democracy which rejected Thrasybulus' proposal to bestow citizenship on all who had fought for Athenian freedom at the Piraeus.

One could hardly find a more significant illustration of the limitations of Greek democracy, and of what Prof. Toynbee calls "the poisonous ingredients with which it had been contaminated from the outset." After 400 B.C., in one city after another, democracy gradually faded out. It had failed because it was inconsistent with the exclusiveness and parochialism of the middle-class citizen, who clung tightly to the privileges which his citizenship brought him, whether in money or prestige. Throughout the fifth century the Athenian middle class had concentrated its energies in agriculture, usury and the paid posts provided by the civil service and the empire. Citizenship was a door which was kept tightly barred against the stranger and the foreigner, who might settle and make money in banking, trade and manufacture, but could not aspire to the full fruits enjoyed by the citizen class. In this exclusiveness the middle class had the support of the workers, who saw in the various forms of state subsidy the one perquisite which divided the poor but free citizen from the slave. Thus, whether rich or poor, the citizen of fifth century Athens felt himself to be the member of a compact, brilliant, exclusive and highly conscious community, which was, in fact, living largely at the expense of the resident alien, the slave and the subject ally.

Sooner or later, however, this exclusiveness was bound to break down. It was a struggle against the tide. And from the fourth century onwards there are clear signs that the division made by the possession of citizenship was growing less distinct. The wealthy on both sides of the line began to coalesce to form a single social group, the bourgeoisie, to whom the old parochial exclusiveness had little meaning; and under Alexander and his successors it was this class which became the driving force throughout the Greek world. To Prof. Rostovtzeff we owe a fascinating description of its achievements during the Hellenistic Age. The bourgeoisie he defines as that section of the population which lived off the proceeds of capital invested in some branch of economic activity. It included landowners and tenant farmers; owners of industrial workshops; owners or tenants of shops, ships and warehouses; moneylenders; and slave-owners, who hired out their slaves for work in ships, mines and workshops, or who let them conduct business directly on their master's own behalf. It was this class that controlled the wealth and the culture of the Greek cities and the monarchies of the Hellenistic Age, having crystallised into a recognisable group in the course of the fourth century.

Since city-state hegemonies no longer existed, it was easy now to treat on terms of friendly equality with the city that would formerly have seemed a potential subject or mistress. Moreover, the new foundations in Asia were free from the old traditions of exclusiveness which had historical roots in the cities of Greece proper. Hence this form of particularism had to and did give way. But vertically the bourgeoisie remained as rigidly exclusive as ever their predecessors were. Indeed, certain new developments of the Hellenistic age tended to accentuate class differentiation. With the increase in the number of slaves throughout the Greek world as a result of the wars of Alexander's successors, society was drawn

out towards greater extremes of wealth and poverty. Having annexed the older lands of the Nile and the Euphrates, the Greeks became acquainted with a more rigid, oriental, caste-system, which had all the authority of antiquity, and seemed more impervious to social change than the forms of society they had known at home. The old antinomy between the town-dweller and the peasant within the ancient agrarian empires of Asia, was now inherited by the successor states of Alexander; and in Egypt, where a unique system of royal monopoly was adapted and perfected by the Ptolemies, a peasant population of legally free *fellahin* filled the role elsewhere assigned to slaves. Barring a few faint notes, which swelled loudest in Judaea, this subject class remained voiceless and unheard; the stream of history passed it by.

Nevertheless the growing polarisation of society eventually made itself felt in a series of class struggles of a new type. Struggles to throw off an effete aristocracy or oligarchy the Greeks had known; the bitterness and resentment of the vanquished can still be read in the pages of Theognis.[3] But now the Hellenistic Age saw fierce conflicts provoked by the basic classes of society, slave revolts like those of Sicily and Pergamum, the Carthaginian mercenary war, and such proletarian movements as that which gave its misguided support to the Spartan revolution of Cleomenes, and prompted the setting-up of the counter-revolutionary Symmachy of Antigonus Doson, an important function of which was to protect the Achaean bourgeoisie

[3] An elegaic poet, born ca. 540 B.C. in Megara, Theognis was driven into exile when the aristocratic party, of which he was a member, was defeated.—*Ed.*

from the spread of Spartan "communism" among the masses in their own cities. This increase of class-war coincided with a decline in the prosperity of the bourgeoisie themselves. "The rapid growth of wealth in the hands of a few members of the class," comments Rostovtzeff, "did not compensate for its impoverishment as a whole. . . ." This was especially true in Greece proper, where an acute problem of depopulation from the end of the third century onwards offers perhaps the clearest indication of general decay. Indeed, just as four centuries later the decline of Italy prefigures the decay and break-up of the Roman Empire, so now mainland Greece offers the first, warning sign of the decline of the Hellenistic World.

This failure of the Greek middle class to preserve and enlarge the democracy it had established, and the gradual accentuation of class-differences and class-conflicts, is an underlying factor easily traceable beneath the general features of social-political and cultural decline. "Greece and poverty," wrote Herodotus, "have always been foster-sisters"; and as a corollary to this Aristotle characterised poverty as the parent of revolution and crime. Continued exclusiveness in a world of poverty could only lead to an explosion and to the chronic *stasis* [revolution, civil war] endemic in ancient Greece; its effects on the quality of social and cultural life had already been catalogued in the sombre pages of the third book of Thucydides. In a community based on the exploitation of slave and neighbour, where the distinction between the "city-state of the sponge" and the "vast military empire of the shark" was to be measured solely by the lack or presence of power and opportunity, where the artistic achievement of the

Athenian Acropolis was made possible only by a tyrannous imposition exacted from unwilling subjects, what hope was there of unity? And what meaning was there in freedom? The Persian and the Macedonian could always find his allies in Greece itself; and later, in the Hellenistic period, the bourgeoisie, in fear of those classes from whose labours its wealth was drawn, would always make common cause with the kings under the slogan of *Homonoia*. In the long run they were prepared to surrender all. . . . All over Greece the upper classes came to terms with the barbarian, and the Greek wars of the second century were all more or less wars of class against class; after the swift Roman victory of 146, Polybius informs us, there was a proverbial saying commonly heard on the lips of his defeated compatriots: "If we had not perished so quickly, we should never have been saved!"

In the cultural life of Hellenic society the poison was also at work, and the havoc it wrought could not long be concealed. Here a single example must suffice. Discussing the collapse of the Roman Empire, Rostovtzeff points to the significance of the wave of superstitions and oriental cults which swept over the lower classes from the east, until ultimately the bourgeoisie and the cultured classes were also submerged and the light of Greek rationalism finally put out. A similar phenomenon accompanied the decline of the Hellenistic world in the third and second centuries; Prof. G. Murray once summed it up as a "failure of nerve." What caused it? Did it correspond to a spontaneous revulsion from rational thinking on the part of the masses? Or did the trustees of Greek culture deliberately "Medise," if we may borrow a metaphor from the parallel sphere of politics? There is no simple answer. Times of stress are always rich in superstition. But the question may also be answered in part, if we consider once more the tragic role of Plato, who, in the *Laws*, deliberately welcomes and inculcates superstition as a mental pabulum not only for the lower classes, but even for the wardens of his ideal state. For the former the old Olympian cults, for the latter the new astral deities are to be an object of faith which may not be challenged. Whether Plato himself believed in either is extremely dubious; despite temperamental differences, his attitude here is fundamentally, if less frankly, that of Polybius, who, two hundred years later, expressed his admiration for the use to which the Roman State put religion, keeping the lower classes in subjection by a judicious compound of terrors and pageantry. Yet to the impartial observer such a renunciation of honest thinking can surely appear only as the blackest treason to that flowering of the human spirit which we call Hellenism, treason, too, in its most gifted exponent, and explicable only as the outcome of a motive of irresistible compulsion. That motive was unquestionably the maintenance of privilege, the preservation of an oligarchic and paternal form of society with power and responsibility concentrated at the top. In the interest of such a social order and its perpetuation Plato is prepared to purge and censor most of the finest products of Greek genius. He had set out with the purest motives; he followed the light as he saw it. But what he did not see was that obscurantism cannot be confined to the lower orders; like a plague arising among city slums, it sweeps outwards and upwards until it has infected every rank of society. When that happens, society must either root it out or perish.

Two issues the generations after Plato never faced: one was the unfettered application of the observational method to the problems of nature, the other the questioning of the basic organisation of society. It is not easy to over-estimate the importance of the teaching of the Academy in turning men's minds away from observation, and inspiring what Glanvill, many centuries later, described as "thinking in the notional way," deduction, that is to say, of the particular from the general, this having first been arrived at on *a priori* principles. Not even Aristotle could shake himself wholly free from this legacy. Correspondingly, in the social sphere, there was no serious challenge to slavery, or to such other concomitant abuses as the inferior position of women. As Rostovtzeff points out, the various utopias of Zeno, Hecataeus of Abdera, Euhemerus and Iambulus were "mere products of theoretical speculation . . . and had no relation to or influence on practical politics." The Stoics began by asserting the equality of slaves and free men; but they never drew the obvious conclusion that slavery should therefore be abolished, and later, in the Middle Stoa, they reverted to the Aristotelian view that slavery was a natural institution. In short, Hellenistic thought remained closely bound up with the patterns of behaviour of the Hellenistic bourgeoisie. The renunciation which Plato was driven to make deliberately and consciously his successors made unconsciously and without an effort.

It seems clear, then, that the increasing economic cleavage of Greek society into rich and poor, privileged and exploited, was a basic factor in both the social-political and the cultural decline which became apparent from the fifth and fourth centuries respectively. This cleavage necessarily raises the problems which were occupying Rostovtzeff's attention in 1926. Why, we must ask, did Greek middle-class democracy stop short? Why was the economic system never expanded to enable wealth, and with it culture, to spread downwards throughout society? Why was the accumulation of wealth in the Hellenistic world never used as a basis for capitalist and industrial expansion, instead of going (as it so often did) into unproductive channels, such as temples, festivals and public luxury? In fine, why did ancient society, having reached a certain point, stop short in its tracks, and then begin to decay instead of advancing towards a fuller democracy based on an increasing mastery over the forces of nature?

Stated in these terms, the problem identifies itself—as ultimately it must—with what is perhaps *the* question of ancient history, namely: What caused the decline and fall of the Roman Empire? The more important contributions to the discussion of this topic have been reviewed in a recent paper by Prof. N. Baynes,[4] and they need not detain us here. There is, however, one point I would make in connection with Rostovtzeff's approach to the problem in his *Social and Economic History of the Roman Empire*. Towards the end of this work the author deals with the theories of certain of his predecessors, dismissing some as untenable, and characterising others as only partial answers; and in

the end his conclusion is *non liquet* [not proved], accompanied by a hint that all approaches have made a definite contribution to our understanding of the problem. In a sense this is true. But what he perhaps does not make clear is that many of these "explanations" are, in fact, symptoms; and though symptoms are essential in a diagnosis, the cause of the disease is usually something quite independent of their sum total.

In particular, Rostovtzeff's approach is handicapped by his unwillingness to admit the priority of any one field or category of human activity—social, political, economic or religious—over the rest. ... This ... postulates a series of parallel, partial causes for any historical event, sometimes linked together mechanically, but never organically; history becomes something amorphous, eclectic; and in view of the "complexity of life" the historian renounces the function which he has claimed from the days of Thucydides, that of explaining not only *how*, but also *why* things happen.

Now admittedly one result of this principle has been that Prof. Rostovtzeff has admirably resisted the temptation which besets the "economic historian" to see an economic cause for every incident, and so to over-simplify the process of history. Indeed, he will command general support in his rejection of Salvioli's theory that the ancient world failed because it never advanced beyond the stage of household economy, or the rival theory of Simkhovitch which puts the root of the trouble in soil-exhaustion. On the other hand, having made these points, he is inclined to assume that he has disposed of the mode of production as a basic factor in the situation. And this is far from being so.

Rostovtzeff's own work makes it clear

[4] N. H. Baynes, "The Decline of the Roman Power in Western Europe. Some Modern Explanations," *Journal of Roman Studies*, vol. 33 (1943), 29–35.

that classical civilisation was at all times based on a technique that was backward not merely relatively to that of modern times, but absolutely; that is to say, the exploitation of nature and the development of natural wealth was at so low a level that the leisure and culture of the few had to be balanced by the toil and want of the many, whether their status was that of poor workman or peasant, serf or slave. The difference between slave and free proletarian was important psychologically; but in Hellenistic times the "hireling for life," as Chrysippus called him, differed in terms of real welfare from the slave only in his "personal freedom and more precarious situation as regards work and food." Thus the intensive exploitation of man replaced, and indeed excluded its alternative—the intensive exploitation of nature. Once slavery has spread from the home to the mine and the workshop, it appears to rule out the development of an advanced industrial technique. For the kind of slaves employed in the big productive processes such as agriculture or mining are not capable of operating complicated machinery or advanced methods of natural exploitation, still less of improving them. Hence slavery militates against the development of mechanical power; and at the same time it brings few advantages in the concentration of industry, and therefore offers little opposition to the tendency of production to fly outwards to the periphery of the economic area. Furthermore, when slaves are there as an alternative, the producer has no incentive to economise labour; and the bargaining power of the poor, free, worker is automatically reduced where the two classes are in competition (as they frequently were in the Hellenistic Age),

and consequently there arises what is today termed the problem of the "poor white."

But equally important is the psychological effect of this social cleavage between those who possess the power and the wealth, and those who actually do the work. More than once Rostovtzeff mentions the "conservative spirit of the Hellenistic period in regard to technical innovations in the field of industry." To speak of a "conservative spirit" is, of course, to define, not to explain; and there can be little doubt that the search for an explanation brings one back immediately to the fact of a well-differentiated class system, which produced an atmosphere wholly unsympathetic to invention and technical progress. Certainly it was the new spirit of the early Greek trading cities, where the power of land was already broken, but wealth was not yet unduly concentrated, which transformed the scientific traditions of the east to create the amazing results of the Ionian Renaissance. Again, the general flux of the early Hellenistic Age, the new cities with their go-ahead "middle-west" outlook, the stimulus of new trade and new ideas, released a fresh burst of creative activity in the late fourth and early third centuries. But as the world settled down in its new shape, classes rigidified again, retardation once more set in: it forms a constant refrain in the work of Rostovtzeff, who indeed emphasises the slow rate of technical progress and the failure to achieve mass production. For this he offers a threefold reason: (1) the local production of manufactured goods, (2) the arrested development of large industrial centres, (3) the low buying capacity and restricted number of consumers. It will be observed that none of these is a primary cause; but the last and most important raises the fundamental problem with which we are concerned here—the bourgeois monopoly of wealth, and so of purchasing power.

If we attempt to analyse further the failure to make progress in technique, we shall find that it links up with the contempt felt by the Greek middle class for manual work of all kinds. That this attitude grew stronger during the Hellenistic Age seems indicated by an interesting fact to which Rostovtzeff draws attention, namely, the disappearance of representations of working craftsmen from the pottery of this period, and instead the depicting of mythological and abstract themes. This pottery is, of course, produced by craftsmen; but the themes the craftsman introduces reflect the interests of his public. Hence it appears that the Hellenistic bourgeoisie, unlike their predecessors, found pictures of craftsmen working either vulgar or tedious. Moreover, there is plenty of other evidence for this widespread attitude. Hasebroek has assembled a number of instances from the fifth and fourth centuries; and Rostovtzeff has himself stressed the significant fact that the Greek bourgeoisie never accepted the *technites*, or member of what we should today term the liberal professions (*i.e.*, civil servants, professional soldiers, teachers, doctors, engineers, architects, sculptors, painters, artists and lawyers), as a social equal. Because these *technitai earned* their living, by practising a skill and for wages, they were regarded as being socially on the level of the artisan. Their incomes were low and they were frequently outside the citizen body, as metics or slaves; their absence from among the solid characters of the New Comedy supports the view that they were not considered respectable.

This distinction, which clearly reflects the bisection of society into two classes with antithetical interests, had disastrous effects in every sphere of life. Prof. B. Farrington has described these effects, at a later stage, on the practice of medicine, perhaps the most realistic and progressive of all the crafts; and at an early date one result was the diversion of scientific thought away from practical observation and experiment, into notional and metaphysical channels, and the consequent check on technical progress.

However, it would be misleading to suggest that there were no exceptions to this rule. In building and engineering the Hellenistic world, like the Roman Empire afterwards, made certain notable advances. Particularly inside the monarchies there was a considerable programme of building, including the construction of roads and aqueducts, and this in turn stimulated various allied crafts. Even more, in the science of engineering, in its relation to warfare, there was constant technical innovation. Vitruvius' account of the rivalry during the siege of Rhodes between the two engineers Callias and Diognetus is an interesting example of the way in which ancient inventiveness could forge ahead where a pressing situation overrode any prejudice against linking up theory and tradition with experimentation and practice. As a result, the architect and the engineer were exceptional, not only in the attitude with which they approached their tasks, but also in the prestige which their professions seem to have enjoyed. Such figures as Ctesibius of Alexandria, Philo of Byzantium and Archimedes of Syracuse, theoretical writers and practical inventors alike, enjoyed a position in society well above that ordinarily accorded to the *technites*.

Yet their exceptional status did not mean that such of their inventions as had no direct application to warfare—for instance, Ctesibius's pump or the many ingenious devices recorded in Hero of Alexandria—were rationally employed otherwise. Indeed, it is perhaps symbolic of the position of ancient applied science that Hero's inventions, far from being used for the benefit of mankind, were employed by the priests of Egypt to simulate miracles, and so, by facilitating a pious fraud on the faithful, to assist in the secular struggle of superstition against reason. . . .

There was no growing demand because there was no large market for the products of industry; and there was no such market because the form of exploitation kept the masses at the level of poverty, and the price of labour cheap, whether free or slave. The modern world has solved a similar dilemma up to a point by exporting its surplus overseas; but this method was not open to a civilisation which was still geographically circumscribed, after absorbing as much territory as it could digest. Moreover, the structure of society *outside* the areas of Hellenism (and later of the Roman Empire) was not such as to provide markets for goods for mass consumption. Accordingly one is here driven to ask: Why then did antiquity never attempt a radical solution to this *impasse?* In short, why was the bourgeoisie not superseded as the governing class in society by a revolt of the oppressed masses? From the Hellenistic Age onwards there were frequent proletarian and slave risings. The part played by social revolution and its threat in the wars of Sparta against the Achaean League has already been mentioned; and later on there are the revolts of Aristonicus at Pergamum, the Mithridatic War, the Sicilian slave revolts, slave risings in Attica, Macedonia and Delos, and the rising of Spartacus in Italy. But a significant feature of these movements is that "in the few cases where social revolution was successful," as Rostovtzeff observes, "this was the result of political conjunctures which prompted the leaders of the day to lend their support to the aspirations of the proletariat." Perhaps the most notable example of this is to be seen in the careers of the Roman *populares* and the use they made of the urban mass at Rome. This constant diversion of the revolutionary movement to serve the interests of someone outside it is only to be explained as a measure of weakness in the movement itself; it is the mark of immaturity and inadequate internal organisation and drive. Hence it never appeared likely that the proletariat would succeed not merely in overthrowing the middle classes, but also in setting up in the place of the existing state a wider social order, capable of conserving classical culture and extending it to a broader section of society.

Indeed it is very questionable whether such a thing was economically possible, without a radical change in the level of production. Technique in the ancient world had never supported more than a minority culture; and though it can be argued, with justice, that this minority culture had always been very wasteful, investing its resources in luxuries and non-productive forms of wealth, this is not to say that with the most careful planning and management the resources and technique actually available would have been sufficient to keep the whole community at a level bearing any relation to classical civilisation as we know it. In any case, if the purely economic problem is most safely left open, there are other factors which wholly rule out the possibility of such a revolution. Even the most effective of the slave-revolts, for instance the Sicilian risings of Eunus in 135 and Athenion in 104 (both of whom made some attempt to plan their resources with an eye on the future), did not reveal a sufficient unity of idea and purpose among the rebels to give any prospect of lasting success. For the general effect of slavery was to split the proletariat, not to strengthen it. There is every reason to think that a proletarian victory, if by some miracle it could have been achieved, would have meant nothing more than a change of masters. In fact, looking back from the vantage-point of the present, we can see that an organised proletariat capable of displacing the bourgeoisie, and both maintaining and expanding civilisation, first came into existence with the industrial revolution, which provided both the improved technique and increased wealth essential to mass civilisation, and also the concentration of the proletariat in factories and mines under conditions which enabled it to attain a community of purpose and a realisation of its own strength.

These conditions never existed in the ancient world; and the Hellenistic bourgeoisie, conscious that it was a question of themselves or nothing, constantly set their faces against any movement designed to secure social readjustment. In this respect their propaganda was consistent with their practice. . . .

Thus the ancient world seems to have been caught in a dilemma. The economy both of the Hellenistic world and, later, of the Roman Empire, was based on a low level of technique and a form of exploitation which neither encouraged nor engendered technical progress.

Moreover, the mental attitude inspired by this system was one which, among the bourgeoisie, turned men's interests away from the creation of wealth to its consumption, which accentuated exclusiveness and class hatred and fear, which on the one hand encouraged contempt for physical work and, ultimately, even for such intellectual work as rested upon it, and on the other hand set up an exaggerated respect for notional thinking —an attitude which led up to and beyond the intellectual treason of Plato; meanwhile, among the workers themselves it induced the slave mentality, the frame of mind which was satisfied perforce with little and fell back on a pattern of behaviour which could only reinforce the contempt in which the middle classes already held those upon whose backs they lived.

Was there any available way out? In this question, as in others, speculation will always busy itself with "ifs"; but the fact that history must face is that throughout the whole of classical civilisation no radical solution was devised for the problems outlined above. Of course the decline was not along a regular downward slope. The expansion of Alexander and his successors, and the consolidation effected by Augustus and Hadrian, each for a time put a brake upon the process of decay and even facilitated a partial recovery. But the real causes were never eradicated, and after a while the decline always set in again. Ultimately the supply of slaves dried up, and the western empire stabilised itself at a low level, its production in the hands of serfs and tied craftsmen, and its government a rigid bureaucracy.

Yet all was not lost. As Prof. Baynes has recently reminded us, the eastern empire went on after the western half had foundered; and even in the west there was never a clear and complete break. Consequently, when the barbarian invasions were themselves events of the distant past, and new towns began to spring up in Europe, inhabited by neither serfs nor slaves, the techniques of the ancient world were there for men to build on. Unobtrusively the craftsmen grouped around manor or monastery had passed their knowledge down from father to son. And so once more, in an atmosphere free from the deadening effect of the ever more rigid class-system of late antiquity, men could go forward to the mastery of nature. With them they bore the full cultural legacy of the ancient world, adapted now to a task from which antiquity itself had necessarily drawn back, but which gave promise of easy accomplishment to the new and fruitful partnership between mind and hand.

The incisive criticisms of ancient democracy made by M. ROSTOVTZEFF (1870–1952) seem to reflect his personal disillusionment with the ability of the masses to govern themselves, a disillusionment presumably inspired (as Walbank noted) by his own experiences with the Russian Revolution. Rostovtzeff was born in Russia but left after the revolution; he lived in America until his death and held a professorship first at the University of Wisconsin and then at Yale University. Among the best-known of his works are *Social and Economic History of the Roman Empire*, *Social and Economic History of the Hellenistic World*, and a two-volume *History of the Ancient World*, from which the following pages are excerpted.*

Political Equality: The Levelling Process

The Greek city-state, in the two centuries of its development, proved unable to create a national union of Greece, and reduced Greece to a condition of political anarchy, which must infallibly end in her subjection to stronger and more homogeneous governments. Apart from the tendency to separation innate in the Greek mind, the blame for this failure lies largely on the constitution of the city-states, and, most of all, on democracy, the most complete and progressive form of that constitution. Democracy in Greece proved unable to create a form of government which should reconcile the individualism characteristic of the nation with the conditions essential to the existence of

a powerful state, namely, civic discipline and a preference of the general interest, even when it appeared to oppose the interest of particular persons or classes or even communities.

The fifth century B.C. was exceptionally favourable for the growth of individualism. The extension of trade, the great technical improvements in agriculture and industry, the supremacy of Greece in the world's markets, her production of oil, wine, manufactures, and luxuries for all those countries to which her colonists had penetrated—such conditions had enabled the Greeks to show their enterprise in the sphere of finance, and to abandon more primitive methods in favour of a capitalistic system and a

* From M. Rostovtzeff, *A History of the Ancient World*, translated by J. D. Duff, vol. I, 2d ed., pp. 315–317. Copyright 1929. Reprinted with permission of the Clarendon Press, Oxford.

production aimed at an unlimited market with a demand constantly increasing in amount. The rudiments of such a system are noticeable at Athens even earlier than this century. The transition to capitalism was made easier by the existence of slavery, as an institution everywhere recognized, whose necessity and normality no one questioned. The slave markets provided slave labour in abundance; and the growth of political anarchy only increased the supply of slaves and lowered the price of labour. But capitalistic enterprise was interfered with by the state: within the limits of small states it was difficult for the capitalist to go ahead: their territory was too small and the competition of neighbours too severe. And apart from this, within each state capital had to fight the socialist tendencies of the government and its inveterate jealousy of all who, either by wealth or intellectual and moral superiority, rose above the general level. Thus capitalism and individualism, growing irresistibly, came into constant conflict with democratic institutions; and the conflict led to utter instability, hindered the healthy development of capitalism, and turned it into speculative channels with which the state was powerless to interfere.

Among the characteristic peculiarities of Greek democracy is its view that the state is the property of the citizens—a view which includes the conviction that the state is bound, in case of necessity, to support its members, to pay them for performing their public duties, and to provide them with amusements. These expenses had to be defrayed by the state either out of the public funds, including its foreign possessions and the tribute paid by the allies, or, if these funds were insufficient, at the cost of the more wealthy citizens. In extreme cases the state resorted to confiscation and requisitioned, on various pretexts, the riches of the well-to-do. When the government sold corn and other food below the market price, or paid the citizens for attendance at the popular assembly and for serving as judges, members of the Council, and magistrates; when it gave them money to buy tickets for the theatre and fed them for nothing in times of dearth—in such cases the usual procedure was to squeeze the rich for the means: they were compelled either to lend money to the state, or to undertake, at their own cost, the management of certain public duties, for instance, the purchase and distribution or sale of corn. They were required also to fit out warships for service, and to pay and train choruses and actors for theatrical performances. Such public burdens were called *liturgiae.*

The same levelling tendency is shown by the state in every department of life. The equality of all citizens was a principle of democracy; and where it did not exist forcible measures were taken for reducing all alike to the average standard, if not to the standard of the lowest citizens. In public life all citizens might and must serve their country as magistrates; hence most of the magistrates were appointed by lot and the method of choice was abandoned. In private life, sumptuary laws aimed at the same object; and equality in morals was secured by laws which prescribed definite rules of conduct. And lastly, in order to preserve equality in matters of the intellect, thinkers and scholars, whose opinions appeared subversive of religion and government, were again and again prosecuted. . . .

Democracy had good reason for prosecuting thinkers and men of learning. For they submitted the city-state to merciless criticism based upon a pro-found study of its essence. Some peculiar social institutions, such as slavery and the isolation of women, were repeatedly dealt with, from different points of view, by Euripides and Aristophanes. There is a remarkable review of Athenian democracy, witty, profound, and, in places, malicious, in an anonymous pamphlet of the fifth century; the writer is unknown, but was evidently an important figure in the politics of the day. But the heaviest blows suffered by this form of constitution were dealt by the sophists and by Socrates. . . . Plato, the disciple of Socrates, and Aristotle, the disciple of Plato, summed up the results of this criticism and investigation: in their political writings they gave an excellent and detailed account of such a constitution in its development and practical working, classified all the possible forms which it might assume, and planned the formation of a new and more perfect city-state out of the elements actually existing in Greece.

The demagogues have often been accused of being the enemies within the gates in Athens. They are considered to have been rabble-rousers who exerted their greatest influence on the Assembly following the death of Pericles. EDWARD M. WALKER (1858–1941) maintains that because of them the measures passed by the Assembly were more radical than the political temper of the Athenian people as a whole. If this is true, was the Assembly really democratic? Walker was a Fellow of Queens College, Oxford, from 1881–1930, and provost of the College from 1930–1933. He contributed many articles on Greek history to the *Cambridge Ancient History*, and his books include *The Hellenica Oxyrhynchia*, a study of Greek papyri, and *Greek History: Its Problems and Its Meaning*.*

The Threat of the Demagogues

Even if Aristotle had given us a complete enumeration of all the measures of reform which were placed on the Statute Book in the second and third quarters of the fifth century B.C., the sum total of these measures would have failed to explain the change from the constitution as it stood in the time of Themistocles to the full blown democracy of the days of Cleon. The explanation is to be sought, not merely in any list of legislative enactments, but also in the change in the conditions, social, economic, and political, of the Athenian State. It may be permissible to look for an analogy in the history of that constitution which is as typical of modern, as the Athenian constitution was of ancient, democracy. No changes of any importance, with the exception of the Articles relating to the Abolition of Slavery, were effected in the constitution of the United States during the first hundred years or more of its existence; yet the whole character of the constitution was profoundly modified in the course of the nineteenth century. When we reflect on the extension of the area of the United States, and on the increase in its population during this period; on the industrial revolution which had transformed a society mainly agricultural

---

* From E. M. Walker, "The Periclean Democracy," in *Cambridge Ancient History*, vol. 5, edited by J. B. Bury, S. A. Cook, and F. E. Adcock, (1927), pp. 106–110. Reprinted by permission of the Cambridge University Press.

into one in which the predominant interests were commercial, manufacturing, and financial; on the influx of a vast foreign population, and on the introduction of railways, steamships, and telegraphs, we need not be surprised to find that, while the letter of the constitution remained unaltered, the spirit in which it was worked was no longer the same. Things have doubtless moved far more rapidly in the modern world than they ever moved in the ancient, but movement there was at Athens in the fifth century B.C., and the character of Athenian society, and of the Athenian State, underwent modification in more respects than one in the period that followed the Persian Wars.

By far the most important of the changes in the character of the Athenian constitution during this period is to be found in the rise of the Demagogues. Hitherto it had been the rule that the political leader should have held office as General, and this meant that he must belong to one of the old families who had a tradition of military skill and command. Shortly before the outbreak of the Peloponnesian War a leader of a new type appears on the scene. He is of humble origin (a tradesman or a skilled mechanic), and he has never held office as General. As yet the popular party had been content to find its leaders among the members of the old families, just as in England after the first Reform Bill the Liberal Party was content to find its leaders among the Whig peers. It was only to be expected that a time would come when "the People" would claim to be led by those who were themselves men of the people. The first demagogue of any importance in the constitutional history of Athens is

Cleon, but it is commonly inferred from a passage in Aristophanes that he had two predecessors, at least; Eucrates and Lysicles. From Cleon to the Battle of Chaeronea the succession is unbroken. The contrast between the new type of political leader and the old is thus twofold. In the first place, there is the social contrast. Miltiades and Cimon, Xanthippus and Pericles, Thucydides, son of Melesias, and Nicias, even Aristides and Ephialtes, all belonged to what may be called the "county families." Themistocles is the one exception to this rule. The demagogues were town-bred men, whose manners and mode of speech were alike offensive to the aesthetic sense of well-bred Athenians. It is a common charge against them that they were violent and unrestrained in gesture; and the fact that in the Old Comedy[1] they are twitted with foreign birth and a foreign accent may possibly find an explanation in the vulgarity of their language and pronunciation.

The second contrast lies in the unofficial character of the demagogue. To Grote the demagogue is "essentially a leader of opposition." He illustrates, for example, the respective positions of Cleon and Nicias by the relations of the Leader of the Opposition to the Prime Minister in the British Parliament. He even goes so far as to excuse the part played by Cleophon in securing the rejection of the terms of peace proposed by Sparta after the battle of Cyzicus[2] on the ground that "a mere opposition speaker like Cleophon . . . did not look so far forward into the future as Pericles

[1] The plays of Aristophanes, for example.—*Ed.*
[2] The battle, in which Athens destroyed an enemy fleet, took place in 410 B.C.; it so buoyed the confidence of the Athenians that they followed Cleophon's advice to turn down the Spartan offer.—*Ed.*

would have done." In short, the demagogue is, first and foremost, a critic of measures, not a formulator of policy. Grote, who was much better acquainted with our Parliamentary system than most of those scholars in other countries who have either accepted his premises or attacked his conclusions, intended the comparison of the demagogue with the Leader of the Opposition as a mere illustration; as an analogy that was not to be pressed. What is fundamentally true in Grote's view is that the demagogue need not, and commonly did not, hold any office whatever. His legal position differed in no respect from that of any other member of the Assembly.

That it was possible for one who held no official position to "exercise," for all that, "by far the greatest influence over the people," as Cleon did at the time of the debate on the fate of the Mytilenean prisoners,[3] finds its explanation in one of the most characteristic principles of the Athenian constitution, the initiative of the individual. To critics of the constitution it appeared one of its gravest defects that any individual citizen had the right to put forward any proposal, however insane it might be. It is true that no decree could be submitted to the people unless it had been sanctioned by the Council, but the liberty of amendment allowed to the Assembly was so large as to render this constitutional safeguard far less effective in practice than had doubtless been intended. In no respect does the Athenian

constitution differ more profoundly, both from the Roman Republic, and from the modern systems of Representative Government, than in this. At Rome the initiative lay with the magistrate, while in a parliamentary system even the Private Member, to say nothing of the individual citizen, has surrendered almost all his right of initiative to the Cabinet. Hence no change in the letter of the constitution was required to enable the new type of political leader to emerge. His influence, however, extended far beyond that of the mere critic. Measures of the first importance could be carried in the Assembly in direct opposition to the advice of the Board of Generals, and if this happened no political crisis was involved. Neither the Board as a whole, nor any individual General, was called upon to resign. Consequently, the policy of Athens might be that of "the Leader of the Opposition," rather than that of "the Cabinet."

Political Responsibility at Athens

It was the rise of the demagogues that first revealed one of the most fatal defects in the Athenian system. There are few constitutions in history that have made more ample provision for official responsibility. By the system of *Euthynae*[4] every magistrate, civil or military, was called upon to render an account at the end of his year of office, and prosecutions for peculation, or other offences, on the part of the official were not infrequent. For political responsibility, however, there was no such provision; indeed, the very theory of political responsibility, *i.e.*, of the responsibility of the statesman for the pol-

---

[3] In the early years of the Peloponnesian War, Mytilene, with most of the other towns of Lesbos, revolted against Athens. When the revolt was put down, the Athenians, led by Cleon, voted to kill all the men and enslave all the women and children (427 B.C.). They rescinded the decree at the last moment, but largely (or so it seems) out of self-interest.—*Ed.*

[4] Literally, the giving of accounts.—*Ed.*

icy which he advocates, was imperfectly apprehended by the ancient mind. Thucydides, in one passage, seems to imply that in his view the responsibility for the Sicilian Expedition lay with the Assembly which had voted it, rather than with the speakers who had advised it. This defective theory of responsibility mattered little as long as the political leader held an office; for, so long as this was the case, the political responsibility was merged in the official, and could be brought home to the statesman because he was also a magistrate. Miltiades could be convicted for his failure in the Parian Expedition [489 B.C.], Cimon ostracized in consequence of his dismissal from Ithome [461 B.C.], and Pericles himself brought to trial for the disappointing results of his plan of campaign in the Peloponnesian War[5], because each one of these was accountable for the execution of the policy which he had himself proposed. But how could responsibility for a policy be brought home to the orator who had proposed it, when its execution had necessarily to be entrusted to others? It was inevitable that the statesman should contend that his policy had failed, not because it was faulty in itself, but because the soldiers, or the envoys, who were commissioned to carry it out had proved incompetent or corrupt. To take a single example from the history of the Peloponnesian War, the first Sicilian Expedition failed because it was bound to fail under the existing conditions, but the penalty for failure was visited, not on Hyperbolus and the other demagogues whose scheme it was, but on the unfortunate generals, Pythodorus, Sophocles, and Eurymedon, who were fined and exiled, after the Congress of Gela in 424 B.C., because they had failed where failure was inevitable.

The rise of the demagogues was itself a symptom of a change in the economic conditions of Attica, which affected the working of the constitution in more ways than one. Down to the Persian Wars the landed interest was still predominant in the state, but in the course of the next half century industry and commerce became serious rivals to agriculture. The centre of gravity was shifting steadily from the country to the town. If we include in our estimate the slave as well as the free and the alien as well as the citizen, we may assume that at the outbreak of the Peloponnesian War the larger part of the population was resident in Athens and the Piraeus, although it is clear from a passage in Thucydides that, if the citizens proper are alone taken into account, the reverse of this would be true. He expressly says that the majority of the Athenians down to the year 431 B.C. still lived in the countryside. The plays of Aristophanes afford ample evidence, if evidence were needed, that the country population was conservative in instinct. It was natural that the small farmer should look up to the wealthier landowners who were his neighbours, and that he should be disposed to follow their lead. No such ties of sentiment could exist between the old families and the population of the town. It was in the urban proletariat that the demagogues found their chief support. Whatever may have been the relative proportion of the rural and urban populations so far as they consisted of citizens, it is quite certain that it would be the urban population, rather than the rural, that would fur-

---

[5] He was deposed from office and fined by the people in 430 B.C.; the following year he was reinstated.—*Ed.*

nish a majority of the voters in the Assembly. The inhabitant of Athens or the Piraeus was on the spot; it would cost him little time or trouble to attend. The dweller in the more distant demes of Attica would hesitate before he sacrificed a day's work on his farm (and it must often have meant two days rather than one), in order to exercise his political rights. When payment was once introduced, the attractions of office, as magistrate, or on the Council, or in the law-courts, would make a stronger appeal to the town than to the country. Even a drachma a day would hardly be a sufficient compensation to the farmer or the fisherman; to the poorer sort of citizens in the City and the Port half this amount proved an alluring bait. It was from this class that the jurors, at any rate, must have been chiefly recruited. It followed that the policy of Athens came to be determined more and more by the votes of the urban population, and that the interests of the country were subordinated to those of the town. Nor can we take the tone and temper of the Assembly in the Periclean Age as a fair criterion of the sentiment of the citizen body as a whole. It hardly admits of doubt that the Assembly was more radical in its views than the people.

GEORGE GROTE (1794–1871) belonged to that unique group of nineteenth-century bankers and statesmen who earned an admirable and lasting reputation for scholarship. His twelve-volume *History of Greece* remains, as it was in its time, an important milestone in the writing of Greek history. Grote was primarily interested in political history; he favored democracy, but without blinders, since his own experience in Parliament (he was a Whig in the era of the Reform Bill) made him keenly aware of the problems governments face. His analysis of the enemies of Athenian democracy reflects what is often true of classical scholarship: however much new material is uncovered, old interpretations remain valid. The selection reprinted below follows his detailed discussion of the oligarchic revolution in 411 B.C.*

The Threat of the Oligarchs

[The disastrous defeat of the Athenian fleet sent to Sicily in 415 B.C. had a decided effect on the internal political history of Athens. The defeat seemed to play into the hands of the oligarchs who were, in any event, consistently opposed to democracy. Alcibiades, who always wanted power at Athens, convinced the leaders of the oligarchic faction that Persia would aid Athens against Sparta if the democracy were overthrown and an oligarchy established. The extremists among the oligarchic leadership included Antiphon and Phrynicus. Their policies, described below, led to the success of the oligarchic revolution and the establishment of the Council of Four Hundred in 411 B.C.]

Thus perished, or seemed to perish, the democracy of Athens, after an uninterrupted existence of nearly one hundred years since the revolution of Kleisthenes. So incredible did it appear that the numerous, intelligent, and constitutional citizens of Athens should suffer their liberties to be overthrown by a band of four hundred conspirators, while the great mass of them not only loved the democracy, but had arms in their hands to defend it, that even their enemy and neighbour Agis at Dekeleia could hardly imagine the revolution to be a fact accomplished. We shall see presently that it did not stand—nor would it probably have stood, had circumstances even been more favourable—but the accomplish-

* From *A History of Greece*, vol. VI, part II (London, 1888), pp. 268–272. Reprinted by permission of John Murray (Publishers), Ltd.

ment of it at all is an incident too extraordinary to be passed over without some words in explanation.

We must remark that the tremendous catastrophe and loss of blood in Sicily had abated the energy of the Athenian character generally, but especially had made them despair of their foreign relations; of the possibility that they could make head against enemies, increased in number by revolts among their own allies; and further sustained by Persian gold. Upon this sentiment of despair is brought to bear the treacherous delusion of Alkibiades, offering them the Persian aid; that is, means of defence and success against foreign enemies, at the price of their democracy. Reluctantly the people are brought, but they *are* brought, to entertain the preposition: and thus the conspirators gain their first capital point—of familiarizing the people with the idea of such a change of constitution. The ulterior success of the conspiracy—when all prospect of Persian gold, or improved foreign position, was at an end—is due to the combinations, alike nefarious and skilful, of Antiphon, wielding and organizing the united strength of the aristocratical classes at Athens; strength always exceedingly great, but under ordinary circumstances working in fractions disunited and even reciprocally hostile to each other—restrained by the ascendant democratical institutions—and reduced to corrupt what it could not overthrow. Antiphon, about to employ this anti-popular force in one systematic scheme and for the accomplishment of a predetermined purpose, keeps still within the same ostensible constitutional limits. He raises no open mutiny: he maintains inviolate the cardinal point of Athenian political morality—respect to the decision of the senate and political assembly, as well as to constitutional maxims. But he knows well that the value of these meetings, as political securities, depends upon entire freedom of speech; and that if that freedom be suppressed, the assembly itself becomes a nullity—or rather an instrument of positive imposture and mischief. Accordingly, he causes all the popular orators to be successively assassinated, so that no man dares to open his mouth on that side; while, on the other hand, the anti-popular speakers are all loud and confident, cheering one another on, and seeming to represent all the feeling of the persons present. By thus silencing each individual leader, and intimidating every opponent from standing forward as spokesman, he extorts the formal sanction of the assembly and the senate to measures which the large majority of the citizens detest. That majority, however, are bound by their own constitutional forms: and when the decision of these, by whatever means obtained, is against them, they have neither the inclination nor the courage to resist. In no part of the world has this sentiment of constitutional duty and submission to the vote of a legal majority been more keenly and universally felt than it was among the citizens of democratical Athens. Antiphon thus finds means to employ the constitutional sentiment of Athens as a means of killing the constitution: the -mere empty form, after its vital and protective efficacy has been abstracted, remains simply as a cheat to paralyze individual patriotism.

It was this cheat which rendered the Athenians indisposed to stand forward with arms in defence of that democracy to which they were attached. Accustomed as they were to unlimited pacific contention within the bounds of their constitution, they were in the highest degree averse to anything like armed intestine contention. This is the natural effect of an established free and equal polity—to substitute the contests of the tongue for those of the sword, and sometimes even to create so extreme a disinclination to the latter, that if liberty be energetically assailed, the counter-energy necessary for its defence may probably be found wanting. So difficult is it for the same people to have both the qualities requisite for making a free constitution work well in ordinary times, together with those very different qualities requisite for upholding it against exceptional dangers and under trying emergencies. None but an Athenian of extraordinary ability like Antiphon would have understood the art of thus making the constitutional feeling of his countrymen subservient to the success of his conspiracy—and of maintaining the forms of legal dealing towards assembled and constitutional bodies, while he violated them in secret and successive stabs directed against individuals. Political assassination had been unknown at Athens (as far as our information reaches) since the time when it was employed about fifty years before by the oligarchical party against Ephialtes,[2] the coadjutor of Perikles. But this had been an individual case, and it was reserved for Antiphon and Phrynichus to organize a band of assassins working systematically, and taking off a series of leading victims one after the other. As the Macedonian kings in aftertimes required the surrender of the popular orators in a body, so the authors of this conspiracy found the same enemies to deal with, and adopted another way

[2] He was assassinated by the oligarchs after, among other things, his reform of the aristocratic stronghold, the Areopagas, in 461 B.C.— *Ed.*

of getting rid of them; thus reducing the assembly into a tame and lifeless mass, capable of being intimidated into giving its collective sanction to measures which its large majority detested.

Demagogues: The Indispensable Counterpoise and Antithesis to the Oligarchs

As Grecian history has been usually written, we are instructed to believe that the misfortunes, and the corruption, and the degradation of the democratical states, were brought upon them by the class of demagogues, of whom Kleon, Hyperbolus, Androkles, stand forth as specimens. These men are represented as mischief makers and revilers, accusing without just cause, and converting innocence into treason.

Now the history of this conspiracy of the Four Hundred presents to us the other side of the picture. It shows that the political enemies—against whom the Athenian people were protected by their democratical institutions, and by the demagogues as living organs of those institutions—were not fictitious but dangerously real. It reveals the continued existence of powerful anti-popular combinations, ready to come together for treasonable purposes when the moment appeared safe and tempting. It manifests the character and morality of the leaders, to whom the direction of the anti-popular force naturally fell. It proves that these leaders, men of uncommon ability, required nothing more than the extinction or silence of the demagogues, to be enabled to subvert the popular securities, and get possession of the government. We need no better proof to teach us what was the real function and intrinsic necessity of these demagogues in the Athenian system; taking them as a class, and apart from the manner in which individuals among them may have performed their duty. They formed the vital movement of all that was tutelary and public-spirited in democracy. Aggressive in respect to official delinquents, they were defensive in respect to the public and the constitution. If that anti-popular force, which Antiphon found ready made, had not been efficient, at a much earlier moment, in stifling the democracy, it was because there were demagogues to cry aloud, as well as assemblies to hear and sustain them. If Antiphon's conspiracy was successful, it was because he knew where to aim his blows, so as to strike down the real enemies of the oligarchy and the real defenders of the people. I here employ the term demagogues because it is that commonly used by those who denounce the class of men here under review: the proper neutral phrase, laying aside odious associations, would be to call them popular speakers or opposition speakers. But by whatever name they may be called, it is impossible rightly to conceive their position in Athens, without looking at them in contrast and antithesis with those anti-popular forces against which they formed the indispensable barrier, and which come forth into such manifest and melancholy working under the organizing hands of Antiphon and Phrynichus. . . .

CHARLES ALEXANDER ROBINSON, Jr. (1900–
1965) was David Benedict Professor of Classics
at Brown University. His works on Greek history
include *Alexander, Conqueror and Creator of a New
World*, the *Ephemerides of Alexander's Expedition*,
and a text on ancient history. The book from which
the following extract is taken is a synthesis of
Athenian life and thought in the age of Pericles—
the point of the highest development of democracy,
but also, as Robinson perceives it, the period when
the constitution was subverted. Is it possible, he
asks, that Thucydides was correct and all power
was really in the hands of one man? And if so, how
was this accomplished?*

The Rule of One Man

There is no doubt that the imperial
tribute made possible at Athens the
erection of the Parthenon and other
buildings, the many festivals, and the
payment for various public services, thus
affording an uncritical posterity, when
motivated by crass materialism, with a
justification for imperialism. When,
however, we turn from the number of
temples built, and the relative ease with
which it was all accomplished, when we
concentrate, rather, on the quality of
the works created, it becomes clear that
neither empire nor great wealth are
necessary for spiritual and intellectual
achievement. For example, Aeschylus,
who was perhaps the greatest of Greek

dramatists, died half a dozen years before the birth of the Athenian Empire.
A decade earlier still, Panhellenic efforts had raised the great temple of Zeus
at Olympia, a marvelous portrayal in
architecture and sculpture of grandeur
itself, and the equal of the Parthenon
in every respect except for certain technical matters.

Creativity might coincide with imperialism, but clearly it was independent
of it. Nevertheless, Athenian imperialism had been born and was long to continue. Nor is there any denying its
magnificent fruits for a limited period.
In Athens itself there was little difference
of opinion about the empire—whether to

---

* From *Athens in the Age of Pericles*, by Charles Alexander Robinson, Jr. Copyright 1959 by
the University of Oklahoma Press. Reprinted by permission.

keep it or not—for the conservatives recognized that no politician could survive who opposed it. Its revenues tempted the masses far too much for that. It was in domestic politics, rather, that a sharp cleavage existed between the political factions. The conservatives held that Athens possessed neither the manpower nor the wealth to oppose herself simultaneously to Persia by sea and Sparta by land, and they therefore urged a close association with Sparta.

The natural sympathies of the Athenian conservatives lay with oligarchical Sparta, and there was, besides, much to be said for their position. In addition to the sturdy maritime empire, Pericles had created an empire by land, destined for a very brief life, but during its existence sufficient to terrify Sparta, its important commercial ally Corinth, and the rest of their Peloponnesian League. Could Athens, the conservatives asked, not only build a greater empire than the Peloponnesians, but also ruin their markets? Eastward, the Aegean Sea was already an Athenian lake, when Pericles seized Pegae, a port on the Corinthian Gulf to which Athens could easily send goods overland for shipment to the west. Worse than that, Pericles seized Naupactus, a veritable Gibraltar at the west end of the gulf, controlling its entrance, so that henceforth the ships of Corinth came and went at the pleasure of Athens. It was at this moment, Thucydides remarks, that the Corinthians conceived an extreme hatred for Athens.

Pericles, on the other hand, maintained that Athens could go it alone and hurt the pride and trade of the Peloponnesians with impunity and, if necessary, fight both Sparta and Persia. The party warfare was understandably fierce, and to entrench his own position, Pericles proposed, first, that the jurors be paid for their service. Juries are probably the cornerstone of any democracy, and at Athens no less than six thousand jurors were selected every year. By giving them a daily wage, Pericles completely democratized the juries, since now even the poorest members could serve regularly. Indeed, the typical juror was an old man, and Pericles' proposal was in effect a form of old-age pension.

Pericles' second proposal was of a different order altogether, though like the first it too was passed. Athenian citizenship, he argued, was rapidly becoming a prized possession, and there would be an advantage in restricting it to as few as possible. He suggested to the Athenians, therefore, that they limit the franchise to those who could prove citizenship on both sides of the family. Five thousand names were now struck eagerly from the citizen lists. This represented a complete reversal of Solon's farseeing reform a century and a half earlier and brings us up sharply against a fundamental question asked by Athenian history. Since Solon was followed by greatness, as Pericles was by disaster, are we to conclude that liberality and breadth of outlook produce the one, selfishness and narrowness the other?

In such ways as we have described, Pericles broke the conservative opposition to him. He was able to do so because, from the time of his emergence as leader of the democratic faction in 461 B.C. to his death in 429 B.C., the Athenians elected him frequently to the Board of Ten Generals, the chief executive body at Athens. Athens now presents the picture of a state where the citizens elected the magistrates—in a word, we seem to have a true democracy—and it is customary to let it go at that, in order that ancient Greece may shine in as bright colors as possible. But we must not gloss over a startling statement of the first importance by Thucydides, that as long as Pericles lived, "Athens, though still in name a democracy, was in fact ruled by her first citizen." What could be the basis for Thucydides' remark, or rather what had happened to make such a remark possible? How could one-man rule have overtaken a democracy?

It is quite true that when they wished, as occasionally they did, the Athenians might not elect Pericles to high office, but generally and enthusiastically they returned him to the Board of Ten Generals. They gained confidence from his earnest manner, the majesty of his person, the dignity of his eloquence, his wisdom and incorruptibility. By the sheer force of his personality and his long experience on the Board of Ten Generals, he dominated the development of Athens during three critical decades.

In effect, this amounted to a perversion of the Athenian democracy, a terrifying fate, almost mysterious in its working, that has so often befallen a democratic constitution. At the opening of the fifth century B.C. it would have been impossible at Athens. In those days, before Marathon, the chief executive body had been the nine archons. Re-election was forbidden. But then, after the victory and as a new Persian invasion threatened, Themistocles thought he saw, as indeed he did, the measures Athens must take for salvation. Driven by both personal ambition and patriotism, as is generally the case with great leaders, he hoped to convince the Athenians that they must build a large fleet. But how was he to do this, since he had already been archon and could never be again?

As a first step, Themistocles decided to destroy, if not the office of archon itself, at least its power. Playing on the democratic temper of the day, he persuaded the Athenians to leave the selection of archons to the gods and to throw the archonship open to the lot. The only result of this could be that henceforth the archons would be nonentities. Inevitably, power at Athens would fall to another executive body, the Board of Ten Generals, where re-election was allowed. It was in this fashion that Themistocles was able to direct Athenian politics during the decade following Marathon, and though our ancient sources fail us in all the details, no other reconstruction will stand up.

At any rate, the archonship ceased to have any importance, except an honorary one, and executive leadership at Athens passed to a different board, that of the Ten Generals. Themistocles' vision saved Greece at Salamis, to be sure, but it was his crafty political maneuvering that upset the constitution. The implications were not immediately realized, but nevertheless the possibility of one-man rule at Athens had been opened.

The Ten Generals at Athens in the days of Pericles were elected, one from each of the ten tribes, by the citizens for a term of one year. Immediate re-election was possible. Their function was far more than a military one since, as the chief executive, they had the duty of presiding at the Assembly, advising the people on a course of action, and carrying out the more important decisions. The members of the Assembly were not experts in government, but ordinary men, eighteen years of age or over, who spent their lives as farmers or artisans or sailors. To guide them in their deliberations could not have been an easy task, especially since self-seeking demagogues might advocate policies in which the magistrates had no confidence. . . .

It is a startling fact that each of the politically dominant people of antiquity, the Greeks and the Romans, should first win at least a theoretical or potential democracy, then lose faith in it, and finally succumb to one-man rule. At the end of the Greek triumph—especially that of Athens—stands Alexander the Great; at the end of the Roman, Augustus. If we could say why faith in the possibilities of democracy was won and lost, not once but twice and forever afterward in antiquity, we would probably have the secret of history's most important lesson.

It is ironical to observe that Rome's "glorious" victory over Hannibal produced a series of almost insoluble problems. The crisis of the long war, with the citizens absent in the armies, meant that the Senate more and more usurped the sole right to rule. When the war ended, and Rome continued to round out her domain successfully, there was a disposition on the part of ordinary citizens to let the Senate remain at the helm. Could the march toward democracy be resumed, how were new foreign influences (especially the sophisticated Greek) to be regarded, what means were to be devised for governing the newly acquired provinces, what was to be done about the growing urban population, composed chiefly of small farmers who had been ruined by Hannibal's devastation? Toward the end of the second century B.C. two brothers, Tiberius and Gaius Gracchus, tried to solve these problems, but when the reactionary senatorial class blocked their efforts, the ancient world was caught up in terrible

conflict. The century-long Roman Revolution, which had begun in the interest of the city masses, ended with the fall of the republic, the establishment of the empire, and the survival of the aristocracy as the dominant class. Does intense party strife produce despair and desire for change, chaos, and the loss of civil liberty?

The Greeks, paced by Athens, had already passed through much the same experience. Liberality bore the twin fruits of democracy and greatness, but when the disappointed, selfish masses were denied full partnership in the developing culture, avaricious leaders were able to drive them to excesses. Party strife, war, despair, and one-man rule followed. The revolutions at Athens and Rome were different in kind, however. The Athenian was a class struggle that tended to bring the riff-raff to the top—which provides its own commentary on the extent of Pericles' success—whereas the conflict at Rome was between aristocratic factions.

There were many reasons why Athens lost the war with Sparta. Party strife, the selfish greed and excesses of the masses, and unscrupulous demagogues stand high on Thucydides' list. But it is equally certain that the Peloponnesian War harmed the victorious almost as much as the vanquished. Despite the great thinkers, such as Plato, who flourished in the next century, individualism and narrow group loyalties began to supplant the traditional devotion to the state. Perhaps this was inevitable because, with the disappearance of the Athenian Empire and its promise of stability, men considered it sensible to think primarily of themselves and the class to which they belonged.

In a sense the fourth century B.C. presents the picture of a society in disintegration, where class feeling and despair, envy of the other man's riches, and the withdrawal of cultivated citizens from political life seem the chief characteristics of the new day. But as faith in the city-state declined, hope of a larger state system, one in which man might move on the level of world rather than regional politics, took its place.

Certain Greek thinkers, for example, thought it a pity that their countrymen did not make war upon a common foe instead of continuing their fratricidal strife. Still others believed simply that the cure of all their troubles lay in monarchy. The two ideas fused in popular thought, and there thus grew up in the Greek world a conviction that the Greeks should unite under a king and make war against a common enemy. It was in precisely this fashion that the fourth century ended, for the Greeks were united forcibly under the Macedonian king, Alexander, in a war against Persia. To be sure, Alexander gave a tremendous impetus to Greek civilization, but henceforth its development was along lines very different from those of Periclean Athens.

MALCOLM F. McGREGOR (1910–   ), presently professor and head of the Department of Classics at the University of British Columbia, taught from 1933–1954 at the University of Cincinnati, where he became professor of classics and ancient history. He has been a member of the Institute for Advanced Study at Princeton (1937–1938 and 1948), and he received an award of merit from the American Philological Association (1954). He is a co-author of the four-volume study, *The Athenian Tribute Lists.* His article, for which Thucydides is the primary authority, is, in effect, an answer to the argument espoused by Robinson.*

▶ ‖‖‖ ## *Thucydides: Oligarch or Democrat?*

Thucydides son of Oloros, I imagine, has enjoyed, during this past generation, a wider reading public than any other ancient historian. He has been the subject of several books and numerous articles. He has been recommended as required reading by Elmer Davis and General George Marshall. To the classical ear, the tone of the speeches, especially those of Perikles, has been reproduced, whether consciously or not, by a Prime Minister of Great Britain and a President of the United States.

The reasons for this persistent popularity are significant and easy to isolate. Of the events of his own time Thucydides writes: "So long as human nature remains what it is, situations like this, or very nearly like this, will some-day recur." He was a citizen of a democratic state involved in a world crisis. His fellow-citizens, the Athenians, were as intellectually active, as politically vigorous a people as we have known, savouring to the full that atmosphere of dissent that we ourselves associate, at least in theory, with democracy. In Thucydides we have the testimony of an acute and competent intellectual, who embodied the qualities of Perikles' ideal citizen, the *politikos.* In addition, he was a painstakingly honest researcher

* From Malcolm F. McGregor, "The Politics of the Historian Thucydides," *Phoenix,* vol. 10 (1956), pp. 93–102; published for the Classical Association of Canada by the University of Toronto Press. Reprinted by permission of the author and *Phoenix.*

and meticulously determined to avoid bias. . . .

. . . I believe that the *History* as we have it—and I grant that it is unfinished—is *essentially* in the form in which Thucydides wanted us to have it. He revised as he wrote, as time passed and made adjustments necessary; much of the composition may have fallen after 404, as he transformed his notes into narrative. The book cannot be divided into isolated chronological strata, representing progressive changes of mind by the author. In it we may properly seek Thucydides' matured political judgements, from which it may be possible to detect his shifts of allegiance, if shifts of allegiance there were. Yet he was not the kind of man who wavered or "bolted" the party; and we should not suppose, by some intuitive preconception, that he was and, to prove it, subject the *History* to distortion.

We begin, then, with the family. . . . Among the branches of Thucydides' family-tree the names of Miltiades, Kimon, and the son of Melesias are conspicuous. It will be instructive to glance at their careers. Miltiades, the leader of the conservative Philaidai, was twice prosecuted by the Alkmaionidai, the handmaidens of democracy, as they have been dubbed, and ended his life in opposition to the popular Themistokles. Kimon son of Miltiades was the advocate of dualism long before Perikles reluctantly accepted it, the rival of Perikles, and a victim of ostracism in 461 as the defender of the Areiopagos against the assault of democratic reformers. Thoukydides son of Melesias succeeded Kimon as the leader of the oligarchic (or conservative) opposition only to fall in the spring of 443 to ostracism and Perikles. This time the issue was imperial policy. Melesias, the father (Thucydides' great-grandfather?), had been an intimate friend of Pindar and had moved in aristocratic circles. . . .

Into this oligarchic Philaid tradition, about 460 B.C., was born Thucydides the historian, to grow up during those exciting years in which Athens was building an empire from whose proceeds Perikles, over the bitter and unsuccessful opposition of the son of Melesias and his party, insisted upon rebuilding Athenian temples. Before Thucydides was out of his 'teens, he was, without question, steeped in the anti-Periklean sentiment of the family and no lover of the democracy.

Among his teachers, in all probability, was the orator Antiphon, of whom he writes in the highest terms. Antiphon, a notorious oligarch who recalls the policies of Kimon and the son of Melesias by his defence of the allies in 425–424, was seriously implicated in the subversion of the democracy in 411.

To this oligarchic, anti-democratic heritage should be added his personal experience and the judgements to which it led. He was, I am convinced, in Athens at the beginning of the war. His command in 424 is our only knowledge of his public service, although it is a fair argument that election to the *strategia* presupposes a competent record. At all events, if this was not his first office, it was certainly his last, for his failure—his inevitable failure—brought him exile from an unsympathetic *demos*. Of the rest of the war he was an observer, a neutral observer, one is tempted to say, who could examine the operations and conduct of the belligerents dispassionately, from a vantage-point that granted the perspective that every historian must have. This explains, in large measure, why Thucydides' *History*, despite the fact that it is contemporary history, is nevertheless a successful work of scholarship.

Not until Book 8, written after a generation of war and a lifetime of thought, does he commit himself openly about government. Of the moderate oligarchy of Five Thousand established in 411–410 he has left this unequivocal verdict: "And certainly, in the first days of this constitution, the Athenians appear to have had their best government, at least in my time; for the blending of the many and the few was temperately effected."

The pattern is consistent; and so are the political views of Thucydides—except that I have not cited all the evidence. An otherwise straightforward story is apparently contradicted by what I have so far suppressed: the estimate of Perikles, the speeches, and, strikingly, the Funeral Speech.

Upon the judgements of the moderns Thucydides' admiration for Perikles has had the greater impact, and it is often assumed that Thucydides was a democrat, that is, a supporter of the Athenian democratic constitution. Or, at least, it is argued that the democratic Thucydides later changed his mind, swayed by the war and his own bitter experience in it, but did little to remove the contradiction from his work. A directly opposite opinion is expressed, incidentally, in a recent review: "Thucydides . . . did not believe in democratic ideals."

Scholars have obviously differed in their views and it may well be that there is an inescapable conflict between the passage on the oligarchy of the Five Thousand, quoted above, and the opinions expressed in the Funeral Speech and the estimate of Perikles. It is of course true that Thucydides' beliefs may have changed. This supposition could be documented by his description of the effects of the war upon the Athenians and their progressive degradation. Yet I cannot find this wholly satisfying, for the tone of the *History* and his own implied judgements do not change at all; the contradiction is not between the early years of the war and the later, it lies among specific passages throughout, of which the crucial one is 8.97.2, without which we might only suspect the existence of the problem. The courageous revival of the Athenian spirit, the stubborn remarshalling of resources, after the Sicilian disaster, as described in Book 8, bespeak a lingering admiration for Athens just before the oligarchic revolution. Of the strictures on democratic government that appear throughout the *History*, early and late, I shall have more to say shortly.

Even more difficult to understand, if Thucydides experienced a political conversion, is the fact that he made no revision of the early passages, he made no effort to tone down the glowing enthusiasm detectable in the Periklean speeches and the estimate of Perikles. This is something to be faced, without flight to the easy sanctuary provided by convenient theories of composition and revision.

What we seek, ideally, is reconciliation of those comments by Thucydides on government that seem to conflict. Our investigation commences with Perikles. From the ostracism of Kimon in 461 to his own death in 429 he was not out of office for more than a year or two; for the last fifteen years consecutively he was elected *strategos*, often, probably, *strategos autokrator*. Long tenure of office, as we know, becomes in itself a ground for criticism and Perikles did not escape. The Olympian figure in Aristophanes surely reflects a phase of contemporary gossip. Today students are often told that Athens was not really a democracy at all; rather, it was a dictatorship. In more fashionable circles, we read of the principate of Perikles, a term which immediately summons Augustus Caesar from the shades. It must be granted that for this view there is weighty authority, Thucydides himself: "What was in theory democracy," he writes, "became in fact rule by the first citizen." The sentence has since been adopted by many as a fundamental text.

Perhaps the most quoted of Thucydides' opinions, it withstands analysis least; a cynic might remark that it is seldom subjected to analysis. Throughout Perikles' tenure of office the *ekklesia* met at least forty times a year. Each spring it elected the generals for the following year. Each year their fellow-citizens examined the qualifications of the generals before they took office. Ten times during the year the *ekklesia* heard reports from the generals. As they left office each year a jury of their fellow-citizens audited their records. One may employ other terms: during Perikles' political life the constitution functioned without interruption and Perikles had to retain the confidence of the sovereign and sensitive *demos* in order to remain in office. Not only was it possible for him to fail of re-election, as indeed he did in 444 B.C.; he might be removed from office, as indeed he was in 430 B.C. In the autumn of that year a disgruntled citizenry deposed and fined Perikles; more than that, they actually despatched a peace-mission to Sparta, *while he re-mained in office,* in direct contravention of his established policy. Now if democracy means and is government by the citizens, if the *ekklesia* decided policy by vote, if free elections persisted at their constitutional intervals, if Perikles was at all times responsible to the sovereign *demos,* and if an unoppressed political opposition survived, as it surely did,—if all this is so, then Athens was as democratic, not only in theory but in day-to-day practice, as government can conceivably be. How such a system can be related to a dictatorship or to a principate is beyond my comprehension. The term principate is particularly unfortunate; for how does Augustus, the prototype, fit the conditions set out in this paragraph, which are not in dispute?

The principle of responsibility was paramount in the Athenian conception of democracy. The mere length of a responsible magistrate's tenure of office should not, by rational judges, be adopted at any time as a criterion of dictatorship. Within our own memories, however, a prolonged term has evoked the same indefensible protest in democratic countries, which should help us to understand, from our own experience, Perikles' position amidst his critics (and admirers) at the beginning of the Peloponnesian War. And nowhere in the modern world is the citizen's control over his representatives more direct and more constant than was the Athenian'. The truth is that Perikles had so won the confidence of his fellow-citizens that they elected him year after year and (wisely, I should say) allowed him, as their elder statesman, to guide them and shape their policies. But that they never surrendered, or diminished, their control of their own destinies is proved no more convincingly by Perikles' failur at the polls in 444 and his deposition in 430 than by his rapid re-election by a repentant *demos* a few months later. Athens remained a full and direct democracy.

But when we fail to discover any incompatibility between democracy and the magistracy of Perikles we are disputing Thucydides' diagnosis, in which, let us mark well, there is no explicit judgement of democracy at all. Elsewhere, however, he does allow himself brief and pregnant comment. In this very chapter, after reporting the fine assessed against Perikles, he goes on, "Not long afterwards, *as the mob is fond of doing* they (changed their minds and) again elected him general." Of events after Perikles' death his words are as follows: "His successors, being more evenly matched with one another and striving, each one of them, to be first, were ready to entrust even the administration of the state to the *demos* to suit popular whim. As a result, many blunders were committed, as you would expect in a great city holding an empire." This chapter, indeed, famous for its eulogy of Perikles, is simultaneously a severe indictment of the Athenian democracy, or, rather, of any form of popular government in a ranking state.

In other passages of the *History* Thucydides' asides are typical of the class-conscious aristocrat who looks down on the *demos*. In his discussion of historical research he complains, "People accept hearsay from one another uncritically," and "So wretched is the general public's search for truth, and they prefer to turn to what is ready to hand." In the debate between Kleon and Nikias, the *ekklesia* eggs on Kleon, "as the mob is fond of doing." Nikias, in a critical moment at Syracuse, regrets that the Athenians "allow themselves to be persuaded by any slander spoken skilfully." Desperate after the Sicilian disaster, "the Athenians, as the mob is fond of doing, were ready to put everything in order in the face of their immediate terror." The sentence is scornful. To Thucydides' mind, characteristically, the *demos* suffered from anti-intellectualism. Witness his tribute to Antiphon, who "was an object of suspicion to the commons because of a reputation for cleverness."

These passages, I believe, have not been relevantly assessed. They make it difficult to call Thucydides a democrat at any time and equally difficult to claim that his political views suffered any fundamental change. Of course, even in 2.65.9 he expresses no approval of democracy. He was, as Wade-Gery so memorably puts it, "caught wholly by the glamour of Perikles." But it was more than glamour, which may be superficial; what he admired was the Periklean state. This state, as (I hope) I have demonstrated, was a democracy; but Thucydides, with his strong oligarchic heritage and his typical distrust of the *demos*, was inherently unable to call it democracy. In praising Perikles, he did not perceive that he was praising democracy. It is this contradiction between his ingrained tradition, in which he believed, and his impartial judgement, based on his personal observation and his innate honesty of intellect, that has confused the interpretation of his political views.

We may find it simpler to understand Thucydides if we recognise that the democratic party at Athens itself developed two wings, one radical and one conservative. Perikles ended his life as a member of the latter. He had had his fling with the radical, aggressively imperialistic type of popular leadership and, by 446–445 B.C., had failed. His failure was remarkable in that he confessed it; he at once abandoned the aggressive policy by land and turned to the consolidation of the naval empire. He was thus able to guide Athens—and so most of the Aegean states—through what was probably the longest period of continuous prosperity and peace that Hellenes could remember. His thoroughgoing reversal I deem the surest evidence of his superior statecraft. This was the man who commanded the allegiance of Thucydides.

With the death of Perikles the restraining voice was gone and the way cleared for the imperialistic radicals, who offered to an avid *demos* a policy that was to prove as disastrous as Perikles had predicted. This transition allows Thucydides to give vent to his natural antipathy to democracy. His indictment of popular government, implied before the death of Perikles, is explicit in his treatment of Kleon, reaches a climax in the shameful words of the Athenian in the Melian Dialogue, and passes inexorably to the final collapse, which Thucydides, who lived to see it, attributes to the folly of the democracy. The state under Perikles, which we, unlike Thucydides, call democracy, Thucydides could endorse with enthusiasm; but Kleon and his kind, in a state in which the machinery and the system had undergone not the slightest change, the oligarchic Thucydides could not stomach. To him Kleon was democracy; we know that Perikles was too. Worse was to come. Alkibiades, that brilliant renegade, borrowed the foreign policies of Kleon; having greater ability and less sense of responsibility, he wrought greater harm.

Yet there were those upon whom the mantle of Perikles fell. Of these Nikias was most prominent. Sometimes considered an oligarch, he was in truth, with his loyalty to Periklean tradition and policy, a conservative, or Periklean, democrat. Of him Thucydides, not surprisingly, writes with a nice appreciation, and in the increasingly grim pages one can detect a real sympathy for Nikias, so honest, so loyal, and, at the last, so ineffective.

The situation after Perikles has been neatly described by John Finley: "Perikles . . . had four characteristics: he could see and expound what was necessary, he was patriotic and above money. Athens' misfortune and the essential cause of her ruin was that none of his successors combined all these traits. Nikias, who was honest but inactive, had the last two; Alkibiades, who was able but utterly self-interested, had the first two. . . ."

This was Athens' tragedy, that she produced no successor who combined all the qualities of Perikles. I have heard it argued that Perikles was culpable for not having left a political heir, that is, that he did not brook rivalry. This, to be sure, is the charge that is commonly levelled at the great man. Apart from the fact that this assumes a principate that never existed and that Nikias *was* his heir, though not his intellectual peer, it is a formidable undertaking to show how one man could suppress others of comparable talent within his own party in a system in which an officeholder was ever subject to discipline and in which a popular assembly provided the ideal arena for the potential statesman to acquire education, training, and reputation. When we bewail the quality of those who received the reins from Perikles, we perhaps fail sufficiently to emphasise the surpassing genius of one who so excelled his contemporaries. "Perikles," Thucydides points out, "influential because of his reputation and intelligence and obvious integrity, was able freely to restrain the people; he led them rather than was led by them. . . . His successors were more evenly matched with one another, striving, each one of them, to be first."

Perikles commanded the respect and the loyalty of men of various political persuasions. Thucydides was one of those to whom the man was more significant than their own partly inherited political convictions. It is a truism that the inspired leader draws support from the state as a whole, irrespective of party-lines. To Thucydides the events that followed the death of Perikles must have come as a bitter, if not entirely unexpected, disappointment; not unexpected, because he had no real faith in democracy and the death of Perikles removed the source of his self-deception. Steadily, as he saw it, the Periklean state was being destroyed. When Theramenes' moderate oligarchy of Five Thousand, with its unrestricted citizenship but restricted privilege, emerged from the revolution of 411–410, Thucydides, reverting easily to his tradition, could follow the dictates of his intellect and pronounce this the best government enjoyed by the Athenians in his time. It is his only categorical judgement on government; it is the key to his political convictions.

One might draw a parallel between Thucydides and the Old Oligarch. The Old Oligarch, it will be recalled, is so named from the nature of his anti-democratic essay written about 425 B.C. He writes, in effect, "I do not approve of democracy, but, if you *must* have it, I admit that the Athenians make a fine job of it." Thucydides, the oligarch born, might have said, "I do not approve of democracy, I see no strength or wisdom in the rabble; but I do admire and will support the Periklean state, which of course is not democracy at all."

We are ready to summarise. Thucydides was reared in the conservative anti-democratic tradition. His orderly and impartial mind was impressed by the genius of Perikles, and so he became a Periklean, though not a democrat; nor could he admit that by so doing he was, in essence, approving of democracy. Later, the oligarchic tradition of his family, that had never been abandoned, reasserted itself, as he saw Periklean ideals forgotten, Periklean warnings ignored. He witnessed, with a brutally piercing eye, what seemed to him the evils of a democracy run to seed, its moral fibre weakening. He ended his life as he had begun it, a confirmed oligarch who had never renounced the creed of his fathers.

NUMA DENIS FUSTEL DE COULANGES (1830–1889), one of the great historians of late nineteenth-century France, cultivated his passion for historical objectivity by basing all his works on a detailed study of primary documents. He devoted himself mainly to the history of institutions, and *The Ancient City*, published in 1873, is still a brilliant work of reconstructing and exploring the institutions of the classical city-state. Do the restrictions on freedom which he describes preclude the possibility of political democracy?*

► # *The Ancients and Individual Liberty*

The city had been founded upon a religion, and constituted like a church. Hence its strength; hence, also, its omnipotence and the absolute empire which it exercised over its members. In a society established on such principles, individual liberty could not exist. The citizen was subordinate in everything, and without any reserve, to the city; he belonged to it body and soul. The religion which had produced the state, and the state which supported the religion, sustained each other, and made but one; these two powers, associated and confounded, formed a power almost superhuman, to which the soul and the body were equally enslaved.

There was nothing independent in man; his body belonged to the state, and was devoted to its defence. At Rome military service was due till a man was fifty years old, at Athens till he was sixty, at Sparta always. His fortune was always at the disposal of the state. If the city had need of money, it could order the women to deliver up their jewels, the creditors to give up their claims, and the owners of olive trees to turn over gratuitously the oil which they had made.

Private life did not escape this omnipotence of the state. The Athenian law in the name of religion, forbade man to remain single. Sparta punished no

* From *The Ancient City* by Numa Denis Fustel de Coulanges, translated by Willard Small. Reprinted as a Doubleday Anchor Book, 1956.

only those who remained single, but those who married late. At Athens the state could prescribe labor, and at Sparta idleness. It exercised its tyranny even in the smallest things; at Locri the laws forbade men to drink pure wine; at Rome, Miletus, and Marseilles wine was forbidden to women. It was a common thing for the kind of dress to be invariably fixed by each city; the legislation of Sparta regulated the head-dress of women and that of Athens forbade them to take with them on a journey more than three dresses. At Rhodes and Byzantium the law forbade men to shave the beard.

The state was under no obligation to suffer any of its citizens to be deformed. It therefore commanded a father to whom such a son was born, to have him put to death. This law is found in the ancient codes of Sparta and of Rome. We do not know that it existed at Athens; we know only that Aristotle and Plato incorporated it into their ideal codes.

There is, in the history of Sparta, one trait which Plutarch and Rousseau greatly admired. Sparta had just suffered a defeat at Leuctra, and many of its citizens had perished. On the receipt of this news, the relatives of the dead had to show themselves in public with gay countenances. The mother who learned that her son had escaped, and that she should see him again, appeared afflicted and wept. Another, who knew that she should never again see her son, appeared joyous, and went round to the temple to thank the gods. What, then, was the power of the state that could thus order the reversal of the natural sentiments, and be obeyed?

The state allowed no man to be indifferent to its interests; the philosopher or the studious man had no right to live apart. He was obliged to vote in the assembly, and be magistrate in his turn. At a time when discords were frequent, the Athenian law permitted no one to remain neutral; he must take sides with one or the other party. Against one who attempted to remain indifferent, and not side with either faction, and to appear calm, the law pronounced the punishment of exile with confiscation of property.

Education was far from being free among the Greeks. On the contrary, there was nothing over which the state had greater control. At Sparta the father could have nothing to do with the education of his son. The law appears to have been less rigorous at Athens; still the state managed to have education in in the hands of masters of its own choosing. Aristophanes, in an eloquent passage, shows the Athenian children on their way to school; in order, distributed according to their district, they march in serried ranks, through rain, snow, or scorching heat. These children seem already to understand that they are performing a public duty. The state wished alone to control education, and Plato gives the motive for this: "Parents ought not to be free to send or not to send their children to the masters whom the city has chosen; for the children belong less to their parents than to the city."

The state considered the mind and body of every citizen as belonging to it; and wished, therefore, to fashion this body and mind in a manner that would enable it to draw the greatest advantage from them. Children were taught gymnastics, because the body of a man was an arm for the city, and it was best that this arm should be as strong and as skilful as possible. They were also taught religious songs and hymns, and the sacred dances, because this knowledge was necessary to the correct performance of the sacrifices and festivals of the city.

It was admitted that the state had a right to prevent free instruction by the side of its own. One day Athens made a law forbidding the instruction of young people without authority from the magistrates, and another, which specially forbade the teaching of philosophy.

A man had no chance to choose his belief. He must believe and submit to the religion of the city. He could hate and despise the gods of the neighboring city. As to the divinities of a general and universal character, like Jupiter, or Cybele, or Juno, he was free to believe or not to believe in them; but it would not do to entertain doubts about Athene Polias, or Erechtheus, or Cecrops. That would have been grave impiety, which would have endangered religion and the state at the same time, and which the state would have severely punished. Socrates was put to death for this crime. Liberty of thought in regard to the state religion was absolutely unknown among the ancients. Men had to conform to all the rules of worship, figure in all the processions, and take part in the sacred repasts. Athenian legislation punished those by a fine who failed religiously to celebrate a national festival.

The ancients, therefore, knew neither liberty in private life, liberty in education, nor religious liberty. The human person counted for very little against that holy and almost divine authority which was called country or the state. The state had not only, as we have in our modern societies, a right to administer justice to the citizens; it could strike when one was not guilty, and simply for its own interest. Aristides assuredly had committed no crime, and was not even suspected; but the city had the right to drive him from its territory, for the simple reason that he had acquired by his virtues too much influence, and might become dangerous, if he desired to be. This was called *ostracism*; this institution was not peculiar to Athens; it was found at Argos, at Megara, at Syracuse, and we may believe that it existed in all the Greek cities.

Now, *ostracism* was not a chastisement; it was a precaution which the city took against a citizen whom it suspected of having the power to injure it at any time. At Athens a man could be put on trial and condemned for incivism—that is to say, for the want of affection towards the state. A man's life was guaranteed by nothing so soon as the interest of the state was at stake. Rome made a law by which it was permitted to kill any man who might have the intention of becoming king. The dangerous maxim that the safety of the state is the supreme law, was the work of antiquity. It was then thought that law, justice, morals, everything should give way before the interests of the country.

It is a singular error, therefore, among all human errors, to believe that in the ancient cities men enjoyed liberty. They had not even the idea of it. They did not believe that there could exist any right as against the city and its gods . . . the government changed form several times, while the nature of the state remained nearly the same, and its omnipotence was little diminished. The government was called by turns monarchy, aristocracy, democracy; but none of these revolutions gave man true liberty, individual liberty. To have political rights, to vote, to name magistrates, to have the privilege of being archon,—this was called liberty; but man was not the less enslaved to the state. The ancients, especially the Greeks, always exaggerated the importance, and above all, the rights of society; this was largely due, doubtless, to the sacred and religious character with which society was clothed in the beginning.

GUSTAVE GLOTZ (1862–1935) held a professorship at the University of Paris and, in addition to making impressive scholarly contributions to his field, trained many leading ancient historians of this century. He is the author of *Ancient Greece at Work* and *The Aegean Civilization*, and in 1907 was editor of *Revue des études grecques*. In the selection reprinted here, he analyzes in detail the constitutional safeguards that the Athenians devised, and shows how they worked in the fifth and the fourth centuries. Glotz then arrives at his answer to the question crucial to an assessment of the failure of Athenian democracy: was it the constitution or was it rather the practice of democracy that was at fault?*

▶ *The Corruption of Democratic Institutions*

Principles of Athenian Democracy

By the middle of the fifth century the democratic system of Athens had assumed its definitive form, the form it was to maintain until Greek independence was destroyed. The value of a constitution, however, depends upon the spirit which animates it. In the age of Pericles Athenian political life showed a perfect equilibrium between the rights of the individual and the power of the State.

Individual liberty was complete. Since the time when Solon had forbidden debtors to vouch for their debts with their person this principle had been given universal application. No citizen could, under any pretext, be reduced to servitude, or subjected to any form of slavery, even though it might be conditional and temporary. Arrest for debt, whether on account of indebtedness to the State or to individuals, existed no longer. The principle of individual responsibility developed in a similar way. The interdiction decreed by Solon profited [primarily] the family of the debtor and, consequently, that of the condemned man. It is true that at the beginning of the fifth century certain outstanding crimes, such as treason, might still en-

* From Gustave Glotz, *The Greek City and Its Institutions*, (New York: Alfred A. Knopf, 1930), translated by N. Mallinson, pp. 128–134; 176–180; 328–332. Reprinted by permission of Routledge and Kegan Paul, Ltd.

tail collective punishment; but the State progressively abandoned that sinister prerogative and, before the end of the century, neither the penalty of death nor proscription involved the children of the guilty man. Thus Attica became the classic home of liberty. There one saw no slaves among the citizens. There even foreigners breathed a quickening air: it attracted the exiles of the whole of Greece, from Herodotus of Halicarnassus to Gorgias of Leontini;[1] and Democritus of Abdera,[2] who established himself there, said that it was better to be poor under democracy than to enjoy the semblance of happiness in the court of a king.

The Athenians, proud as they were of being free citizens, were perhaps still prouder of being equal citizens. Equality was for them the condition of liberty; it was, indeed, because they were all brothers, born of a common mother, that they could be neither the slaves nor the masters of one another. The only words which serve in their language to distinguish the republican regime from all others were *isonomia*, equality before the law, and *isegoria*, equal right of speech. So far from titles of nobility existing, even family names were ignored, and every Athenian without distinction coupled with his own name the name of his deme. At the most people of high birth might indulge in the luxury of perpetuating the name of their father; . . . the State did not recognize families but only individuals who were all of equal worth. All had the same rights. They could enter the Assembly to speak, if they wished, and to vote; for the representative system did not exist and would have seemed an oligarchical restriction of *isegoria*. They could sit in the Heliaea as judges when they had qualified in age. They could present themselves as candidates for the Council and other offices, according to the constitutional forms: they were by turns compelled to obey and permitted to command. They took part in public festivals, processions, games, theatrical representations without discrimination save for the precedence accorded to magistrates. It was equality which the Athenians rated above everything in their constitution. "Advancement in public life," they said, "falls to reputation for capacity, class considerations not being allowed to interfere with merit; nor again does poverty bar the way, if a man is able to serve the state he is not hindered by the obscurity of his condition." . . .

The direct government of the people necessarily turned to the advantage of the majority. But, so long as Pericles was alive, the Athenians did not confuse the mass of individual interests with the common interest. The obligations of the city towards its citizens were surpassed by those of the citizens towards the city. And thus they were undertaken readily.

It was not a tacit and vague contract which bound the Athenian. When he attained his majority, before being enrolled on the register which gave him citizenship he solemnly took the civic oath. Everywhere in Greece, according to Xenophon, the law exacted a similar oath. The young Athenians swore it in the temple of Agraulos. Of the formula in use in the fifth century we know only a single example, that "of recognizing

[1] A famous sophist and orator, ca. 483–376 b.c.—*Ed.*

[2] A philosopher and teacher (ca. 460–370 b.c.) who made outstanding contributions to Epicurean physics.—*Ed.*

no bounds to Attica save beyond the corn and barely fields, the vineyards and the olive groves." But we have fuller knowledge of the fourth century which must on the whole have conformed to tradition. The scene was not lacking in grandeur. The *epheboi*[3] received their armour in the presence of the Five Hundred and, with hands outstretched above the altar, uttered these words:

"I will not dishonour these sacred arms; I will not abandon my comrade in battle; I will fight for my gods and my hearth single-handed or with my companions. I will not leave my country smaller, but I will leave it greater and stronger than I received it. I will obey the commands which the magistrates in their wisdom shall give me. I will submit to the existing laws and to those that the people shall unanimously make: if anyone shall attempt to overthrow these laws or disobey them, I will not suffer it, but I will fight for them, whether single-handed or with my fellows. I will respect the worship of my fathers."

Such were the obligations which the citizens had to recognize before being invested with rights; such were the vows which renewed year by year before the gods the omnipotence of the city.

This omnipotence was wielded by the whole body of citizens in a democracy. The constitutional theory of Athenian democracy was very simple; it can be expressed in a single phrase: the people is sovereign. Whether it sat in the Assembly or in the courts it was absolute sovereign in all that concerned the city. A political principle, however, in all times and places, lends itself to various interpretations and gains precise meaning only in practice. The contempora-

ries of Herodotus employed the same formula as did those of Aristotle and Demosthenes, but they neither understood it nor applied it in the same fashion. In the fourth century the principle: "the people has the right to do what pleases it," was pushed to its furthest limits; it was even sovereign over the laws. . . . In the fifth century it was king, but it was not yet tyrant. It admitted that there were limits to the arbitrary power of the majority. Of the Athenians of this time, as of the Spartans, one can say both of their public and private life: "They are free but they have not an absolute freedom: for above them is a master, the law."

The *graphe paranomon*[4] curbed the enthusiasms of the Ecclesia, as well as the excesses of the demagogues. Even after the death of Pericles it remained efficacious. One day, in tragic circumstances, the people refused to heed it; but they were not slow to perceive their error. It happened in 406 during the terrible trial of the generals who had returned victors from Arginusae. In the midst of heated passions, one courageous citizen attempted to suspend the proceedings, sanctioned by a decree of the Council and the people, by raising the plea of illegality. The crowd protested that it was "monstrous to deprive the people of its power of doing what it pleased." . . . It was in vain that certain members of the bench, Socrates among them, protested against putting the matter to the vote; they yielded to threats, Socrates alone excepted; the resolution was adopted, the accused were con-

[3] Young men who had reached the age of eighteen and were ready for military training. —*Ed.*

[4] An action at law under which an indictment was possible for bringing measures before the Assembly which contravened existing laws; it was usually directed against the person who had moved the resolution. The details are explained more fully throughout the article.—*Ed.*

demned to death and led out to execution. But a little later the Athenians repented: they arraigned by a decree of impeachment those who had deceived the people, and the principal culprit was to die of starvation, detested of all. This exception is excellent proof of the power of the rule: in the fifth century popular sovereignty was something other than arbitrary power, than tyranny. Democracy must have for foundation respect for the law. . . .

Whatever charges one may bring against the Athenian multitude, liable as it was to be carried away by the seductive enticements of orators, it was nevertheless for that same multitude that were evolved those maxims on country, on law, on liberty, equality and philanthropy which have lost nothing of their grandeur and their beauty although they have become commonplaces of the moral heritage of mankind. If it is true, as Aristotle would have it, that the perfect city is that in which all the members scrupulously fulfil their duty as citizens, although obviously all could not be good men, Athens at least approached to that perfection in the time of Pericles, before free play was given to the caprices of the individual and public morality allowed to sink to the level of private morality.

To appreciate properly the role of the Assembly one must, therefore, clearly distinguish between the fifth and the fourth centuries. That distinction is strikingly revealed by a scrutiny of the list of leaders of the Athenian people in the two eras. The amorphous mass had its guiding spirit. There was an almost unbroken chain of party leaders who, by the majority which they commanded, were enabled to exercise a kind

of special magistracy not to be found in the constitution, a hegemony based on persuasion. Though without official title this person filled the position of first minister of the democracy; he was the *prostates* [leader] of the *demos*. Surrounded by his supporters, he defended his programme against the leader of the opposing party and remained master of the government so long as he succeeded in gaining the assent of the Ecclesia for his proposals. In periods when the people was excited by great questions of general, of national, interest it selected its proxy for preference from the *strategoi*[5] responsible for the supervision of foreign policy; it chose him usually from illustrious families, from those which could boast of numerous ancestors and possessed large estates. Cimon the son of Miltiades and the Alcmaeonid Pericles, both great proprietors, are remarkable examples of those *strategoi* who, as *prostatai*, directed the government of the fifth century. Their successors were merchants and traders, not the sausage-seller whom Aristophanes ridicules, but Lysicles the sheep dealer, Cleon the tanner, Cleophon the maker of musical instruments, Hyperbolus the lamp maker: these men represented during the Peloponnesian war a class whose private interests did at least coincide with those of the republic, since in endeavouring to maintain the economic supremacy of their city they sought to protect its maritime empire. In short, the popular Assembly of Athens chose its leaders no more ill-advisedly than do so many of our modern assemblies which emanate from the people by election.

It knew how to protect itself against

[5] Board of Ten Generals with magisterial duties as well; they were elected *by vote* annually and could be re-elected.—*Ed.*

its own impulses. . . . In the fifth century the need for regular and permanent means for effecting the modification of existing laws or the adoption of new laws was not yet felt. . . . Each time that democracy was restored after an oligarchical revolution it appointed a committee of *nomothetai*[6] to select from the laws, conjointly with the Boule [council], those which ought to be abrogated and those which ought to be retained; it was in this way that the *nomothetai* functioned after the fall of the Four Hundred, from 410 to 404, and then after the fall of the Thirty from 403 to 399. But the *nomothetai* of the fifth century . . . differed greatly from the *nomothetai* who, during a large part of the fourth century, were to act as a brake upon the legislative power of the Assembly. At this time they were never more than auxiliaries charged by the people itself with a temporary and special task.

It was to another institution, a judicial institution, that the wisdom of an earlier generation looked for confining in practice the omnipotence of the Ecclesia within just limits. Such was the service which the public action against illegal proposals, the *graphe paranomon*, rendered. In fact this process was, by its origins, its procedure and its sanctions, one of the most formidable weapons at the disposal of the criminal law of Athens.

In early times the laws bestowed by the gods were protected by the sacred power of the curse. When written laws came into being they had for guardian the most august tribunal of all, the one which was invested with essentially religious functions, namely the Areopagus. Then came the reform of Ephialtes[7] which divested the Areopagus of all the functions which made it the guardian of the constitution. It was then that democracy, no longer finding an external check, imposed one upon itself. The first use which it made of its sovereignty was to confine it within insuperable barriers.

Every citizen might become the protector of the laws by bringing an action against the author of an unlawful motion and even against the president who had not refused to put it to the vote. The accuser had to bring forward his complaint in writing, and to indicate the law which he considered had been violated. He might announce his intention upon oath . . . in the Assembly of the people, before or after the vote upon the provisions which he judged illegal. This official declaration had the effect of suspending the validity of the decree until after judgment had been given. The tribunal, composed of a thousand jurors at least and sometimes of six thousand, sat under the presidency of the *thesmothetai*.[8] Any motion might be attacked on the ground of error in form: it was sufficient that the severe rules of procedure had not been meticulously observed. A decree was illegal if it had been submitted to the Assembly without having been previously examined and reported upon by the Council or without having been included in the order of the day. . . . A law was illegal if it was not proposed as the result of a vote expressed in the first assembly of the year,

---

6 In 410 B.C. *nomothetai* were appointed to revise and publish the laws of the democracy. It was a specially constituted committee, but usually, whenever the Assembly decided that laws needed changing, *nomothetai* were selected from among the jurors.—*Ed.*

7 Ephialtes immediately preceded Pericles as leader of the democrats; the reform of the Areopagus was in 461 B.C.—*Ed.*

8 Officials who, in this context, recorded legal decisions.—*Ed.*

and if it had not been displayed in due time and place. Still more serious, as one might expect, was the illegality which arose not from form but from substance. If it was a decree which was in question the accuser was not debarred from urging the evil which would result from it, in order to prejudice the people against the accused; but he was obliged to establish beyond doubt that the decree was in contradiction of existing laws. If a law was concerned, anyone was allowed to demand reparation for the harm done to the republic, by having recourse to a special action . . . ; but, with the *graphe paranomon*, the accusation could only be made in connection with a new law which was in contradiction to a law which had not been abolished. Thus all those whose names were inscribed on a decree issued by the Ecclesia or on a law adopted by the *nomothetai* were under a grave responsibility. The punishment for illegality depended upon the tribunal: it was usually a comparatively heavy fine; but sometimes it was the penalty of death. After three condemnations on the score of illegality the right of making any proposal in the Assembly was forfeited. For the author of an illegal motion prescription was acquired at the end of a year; but for the motion itself there was no prescription, it might always be annulled by a sentence of the tribunal.

Thus, as we see, Athens knew how to prevent its citizens from abusing their right of initiative and, as a consequence, restrained in practice the legislative power of democracy. . . .

The Assembly of the People in the Fourth Century

The Assembly of the people could not remain what it had been before the Peloponnesian war and the oligarchic *coups d'état*. In so far as history admits of such lines of demarcation the archonship of Euclides (403–402) marks, from all points of view, a beginning and an end. From this moment the Ecclesia was to exercise a power more and more "tyrannical," but by making private interests prevail more and more over general welfare: in such a way that the city was never to have appeared so powerful as in the time when individuals, by exploiting it, were preparing its destruction.

Popular sovereignty presented a curious spectacle in the fourth century. It was constantly vacillating between the absolutist tendency which was natural to it and an hereditary craving to oppose the laws to the caprices of decrees.

The public action against illegality, the *graphe paranomon*, had been in former days the principal defence of the democratic constitution. A double experience had shown that the partisans of oligarchy could only seize power by overthrowing this obstacle. Their decisive defeat placed the institution above attack. But at the time when it became unassailable, under the archonship of Euclides himself, a general revision of the laws made it less necessary. Thenceforward it suffered abuse in the struggle of parties. In place of assuring by direful threats supreme protection to the constitution, it became merely a commonplace weapon in the hands of antagonists; . . . soon it became blunted and bent. It was still capable of inflicting death, while it could also be used to inflict an ordinary fine of twenty-five drachmas. Here is a very characteristic instance: a party leader, Aristophon of Azenia, had to defend himself against the accusation of illegality seventy-five times. The result was that the *graphe paranomon*, without preventing the Ecclesia from legislating at random, was an obstacle to wise innovations as well as to foolish, a shackle on that liberty of speech of which the citizens were so proud.

Another process, it seems, might have been able to supplement the *graphe paranomon*: viz. the *eisangelia*,[9] but it too underwent the same degradation. In the fifth century it was intended to repress crimes not provided for by the laws and dangerous to the safety of the State, treason and high treason, including attempts to overthrow democratic government by words or deeds. Laws being lacking the tribunals could not take direct cognizance of these: it was for the Assembly of the people and the Council to take necessary measures for public safety. It involved such severe penalities that the accused did not wait for judgment before exiling themselves. The people clung to this institution, which it attributed to Solon, and which gave a terrible efficacy to its power of supreme justice. It was abolished at the same time as the action against illegality by the Four Hundred, and probably by the Thirty. Not only was it restored under the archonship of Euclides, but a law was then promulgated which, without formally defining it, enumerated the cases in which it was applicable according to precedents. This apparent limitation was to no purpose. By a series of assimilations the Athenians came to treat as attempts against the republic crimes, delinquencies or simple contraventions which bore no relation to the acts legally susceptible

to process by *eisangelia*. Hyperides[10] protested against such abuses and quoted examples which he rightly held up to ridicule: Lycophron was accused by *eisangelia* for having persuaded a woman to be unfaithful to her husband; Agasicles for having been enrolled in a deme not his own; Diognis and Antidorus for having hired out some flute players at more than the legal rate; Euxenippus for having made a false statement as to a dream he had in a temple. Here again a part of the framework of the city was deranged by political hatreds.

What means, then, were to be adopted to prevent illegal proposals from flooding the city? Men remembered the commissions of *nomothetai* who had restored the laws of democracy after the disturbances of 410 and 403. They had been invested with extraordinary powers because of exceptional circumstances; they were now made a regular institution. The existence of this new type of *nomothetai* is proved for the period from the speech of Demosthenes against Leptines in 355–354 to an inscription which bears the date 329–328. In this case we see the people deliberately stripping itself of legislative power, in order to escape the temptation of abusing it. The principle is plain: "no existing law may be abolished save by the authority of the *nomothetai*."

In the first session of the year, therefore, on the 11th of Hecatombeion,[11] the Assembly had to vote on all the laws . . . to ascertain if there was need to abrogate any of them. . . . If the majority

---

[9] An impeachment or trial before a political body, a denunciation.—*Ed.*

[10] A speech-writer and, more prominently, a prosecutor at public trials. He lived from 389–332 B.C.—*Ed.*

[11] Hecatombeion corresponds approximately to our month of July.—*Ed.*

voted for a revision every citizen was free to propose new provisions in the matter in dispute, on condition that he placed his proposal on the pedestals of the eponymous heroes and recognized his responsibility by attaching his name to it. At the fourth ordinary session of the first prytany[12] a decree fixed the number of *nomothetai* called upon to sit, the duration of their office, the procedure they were to follow, the salaries they were to be paid, and drew up their programme, indicating the provisions to be modified or completed eventually. The Assembly then gave its instructions to the *nomothetai*; further, it named four or five *synegoroi* or *syndikoi*[13] whose business it was to defend before them the laws in question. But, once having appointed its representatives, its role was finished, its power exhausted.

Henceforth the legislative people was no longer the Ecclesia but the tribunal of *nomothetai*. They were chosen, to the number of five hundred and one or a thousand and one, from the sworn heliasts, men of age and experience. They were summoned by the *prytaneis* and had their own standing orders. . . . It was not a question of deliberating among themselves, but of hearing a suit which was tried in their presence and of which they were the judges. The *synegoroi* took the defence for the law impugned, while the author of the new law demonstrated its superiority. After that the *epistates*[14] put first the one law

and then the other to the vote of the tribunal. The one which obtained the most votes was *ipso facto* valid. Without further formalities, . . . it was transcribed by the public secretary of the archives, to be classed among the documents having the force of law.

In the texts which have come down to us *nomothesia* was applied in two cases: it legalized decrees which, in the past year, had sanctioned expenses not provided for in the budgetary law; and it authorized changes made in the sacred laws, for example in the ordinances relating to the first-fruits of Eleusis and the feast of Amphiaraus. But there seems no reason why it should not have been applied to many other classes. It is to be presumed that the procedure had a general application.

What is the reason for Aristotle's total neglect of it in his description of the Athenian constitution? Was it, as has been maintained, because the master left everything concerning legislation to his disciple Theophrastus, who did, indeed, write a treatise on the *Laws*? No; for in that case he would have been guilty of wittingly falsifying the picture which he was drawing, for the lack of a word, which would have sufficed to bring it into focus. Moreover, in the *Politics*, not only does he include legislative power in sovereignty, but also he frequently criticizes Athenian democracy for legislating by decrees. The reason must, therefore, be that *nomothesia* in his eyes was of no very great importance and that the decisions of the *nomothetai*, dignified though they were by more complicated formalities, were of the same order as the decrees of the Ecclesia. The best intentions, the justest ideas avail nothing against habits of license and arbitrariness. *Quid leges sine moribus?*

---

[12] One of ten committees of The Athenian Boule (Council), each sitting for one-tenth of the year, and each consisting of fifty members (*prytaneis*) .—*Ed.*

[13] Public advocates who represented the State. —*Ed.*

[14] Chosen by lot from among the *prytaneis*, the *epistates* presided over the Council and the Assembly.—*Ed.*

PLATO (427–347 B.C.) believed that one of the primary reasons the democracy failed was that decisions were made by an unenlightened majority. In the *Gorgias*, he argues that even Athens' greatest statesmen were unable to improve the people. Plato was born in Athens of aristocratic parents; he grew up during the Peloponnesian War and therefore witnessed first-hand the excesses of radical democracy, as well as heard and recorded Socrates' objections to them. When Socrates was condemned and executed in 399 B.C. by the democracy that was restored after the oligarchic revolution, Plato gave up all thought of an active political career; the *Gorgias* contains a vindication of that decision.*

The Unenlightened Majority

soc. And now, most excellent sir, since you are yourself just entering upon a public career, and are inviting me to do the same, and reproaching me for not doing it, shall we not inquire of one another: Let us see, has Callicles ever made any of the citizens better? Is there one who was previously wicked, unjust, licentious, and senseless, and has to thank Callicles for making him an upright, honourable man, whether stranger or citizen, bond or free? Tell me, if anyone examines you in these terms, Callicles, what will you say? What human being will you claim to have made better by your intercourse? Do you shrink from answering, if there really is some

work of yours in private life that can serve as a step to your public practice?

CALL. You are contentious, Socrates!

soc. No, it is not from contentiousness that I ask you this, but from a real wish to know in what manner you can imagine you ought to conduct yourself as one of our public men. Or can it be, then, that you will let us see you concerning yourself with anything else in your management of the city's affairs than making us, the citizens, as good as possible? Have we not more than once already admitted that this is what the statesman ought to do? Have we admitted it or not? Answer. We have: I will answer for you. Then if this is what

* Plato, *Gorgias*, translated by W. R. M. Lamb (Cambridge, Mass.: Harvard University Press, 1925). Reprinted by permission of the publishers from the Loeb Classical Library.

the good man ought to accomplish for his country, recall now those men whom you mentioned a little while ago, and tell me if you still consider that they showed themselves good citizens—Pericles and Cimon and Miltiades and Themistocles.

CALL. Yes, I do.

SOC. Then if they were good, clearly each of them was changing the citizens from worse to better. Was this so, or not?

CALL. Yes.

SOC. So when Pericles began to speak before the people, the Athenians were worse than when he made his last speeches?

CALL. Perhaps.

SOC. Not "perhaps," as you say, excellent sir; it follows of necessity from what we have admitted, on the assumption that he was a good citizen.

CALL. Well, what then?

SOC. Nothing: but tell me one thing in addition,—whether the Athenians are said to have become better because of Pericles, or quite the contrary, to have been corrupted by him. What I, for my part, hear is that Pericles has made the Athenians idle, cowardly, talkative, and avaricious; by starting the system of public fees.[1]

CALL. You hear that from the folk with battered ears,[2] Socrates.

SOC. Ah, but what is no longer a matter of hearsay, but rather of certain knowledge, for you as well as for me, is that Pericles was popular at first, and the Athenians passed no degrading sentence upon him so long as they were "worse"; but as soon as they had been

[1] This refers especially to the payment of dicasts or jurors, introduced by Pericles in 462–461 B.C.
[2] *i.e.* people who show their Spartan sympathies by an addiction to boxing.

made upright and honourable by him, at the end of our Pericles' life they convicted him of embezzlement, and all but condemned him to death, clearly because they thought him a rogue.

CALL. What then? Was Pericles a bad man on that account?

SOC. Well, at any rate a herdsman in charge of asses or horses or oxen would be considered a bad one for being like that—if he took over animals that did not kick him or butt or bite, and in the result they were found to be doing all these things out of sheer wildness. Or do you not consider any keeper of any animal whatever a bad one, if he turns out the creature he received tame so much wilder than he found it? Do you, or do you not?

CALL. Certainly I do, to oblige you.

SOC. Then oblige me still further by answering this: is man also one of the animals, or not?

CALL. Of course he is.

SOC. And Pericles had charge of men?

CALL. Yes.

SOC. Well now, ought they not, as we admitted this moment, to have been made by him more just instead of more unjust, if he was a good statesman while he had charge of them?

CALL. Certainly.

SOC. And the just are gentle, as Homer said. But what say you? Is it not so?

CALL. Yes.

SOC. But, however, he turned them out wilder than when he took them in hand, and that against himself, the last person he would have wished them to attack.

CALL. You wish me to agree with you?

SOC. Yes, if you consider I am speaking the truth.

CALL. Then be it so.

SOC. And if wilder, more unjust and worse?

CALL. Be it so.

SOC. Then Pericles was not a good statesman, by this argument.

CALL. You at least say not.

SOC. And you too, I declare, by what you admitted. And now about Cimon once more, tell me, did not the people whom he tended ostracize him in order that they might not hear his voice for ten years? And Themistocles, did they not treat him in just the same way, and add the punishment of exile? And Miltiades, the hero of Marathon, they sentenced to be flung into the pit, and had it not been for the president, in he would have gone. And yet these men, had they been good in the way that you describe them, would never have met with such a fate. Good drivers, at any rate, do not keep their seat in the chariot at their first race to be thrown out later on, when they have trained their teams and acquired more skill in driving! This never occurs either in charioteering or in any other business; or do you think it does?

CALL. No, I do not.

SOC. So what we said before, it. seems, was true, that we know of nobody who has shown himself a good statesman in this city of ours. You admitted there was nobody among those of the present day, but thought there were some amongst those of former times, and you gave these men the preference. But these we have found to be on a par with ours of the present day; and so, if they were orators, they employed neither the genuine art of rhetoric—else they would not have been thrown out—nor the flattering form of it.

CALL. But still there can be no suggestion, Socrates, that any of the present-day men has ever achieved anything like the deeds of anyone you may choose amongst those others.

SOC. My admirable friend, neither do I blame the latter, at least as servants of the state; indeed, I consider they have shown themselves more serviceable than those of our time, and more able to procure for the city the things she desired. But in diverting her desires another way instead of complying with them—in persuading or compelling her people to what would help them to be better—they were scarcely, if at all, superior to their successors; and that is the only business of a good citizen. But in providing ships and walls and arsenals, and various other things of the sort, I do grant you that they were cleverer than our leaders. Thus you and I are doing an absurd thing in this discussion: for during all the time that we have been debating we have never ceased circling round to the same point and misunderstanding each other. I at all events believe you have more than once admitted and decided that this management of either body or soul is a twofold affair, and that on one side it is a menial service, whereby it is possible to provide meat for our bodies when they are hungry, drink when thirsty, and when they are cold, clothing, bedding, shoes, or anything else that bodies are apt to desire: I purposely give you the same illustrations, in order that you may the more easily comprehend. For as to being able to supply these things, either as a tradesman or a merchant or a manufacturer of any such actual things—baker or cook or weaver or shoemaker or tanner—it is no wonder that a man in such capacity should appear to himself and his neighbours to be a minister of the body; to every one, in fact, who is not aware that there is besides all these an art of gymnastics and medicine which really is, of course, ministration to the body, and which actually has a proper claim to rule over all those arts and to make use of their works, because it knows what is wholesome or harmful in meat and drink to bodily excellence, whereas all those others know it not; and hence it is that, while those other arts are slavish and menial and illiberal in dealing with the body, gymnastics and medicine can fairly claim to be their mistresses. Now, that the very same is the case as regards the soul you appear to me at one time to understand to be my meaning, and you admit it as though you knew what I meant; but a little later you come and tell me that men have shown themselves upright and honourable citizens in our city, and when I ask you who, you seem to me to be putting forward men of exactly the same sort in public affairs; as if, on my asking you who in gymnastics have ever been or now are good trainers of the body, you were to tell me, in all seriousness, "Thearion, the baker, Mithaecus, the author of the book on Sicilian cookery, Sarambus, the vintner—these have shown themselves wonderful ministers of the body; the first providing admirable loaves, the second tasty dishes, and the third wine." Now perhaps you would be indignant should I then say to you: "Sir, you know nothing about gymnastics; servants you tell me of, and caterers to appetites, fellows who have no proper and respectable knowledge of them, and who peradventure will first stuff and fatten men's bodies to the tune of their praises, and then cause them to lose even the flesh they had to start with; and these in their turn will be too ignorant to cast the blame of their maladies and of their loss of original weight upon their regalers, but any people who chance to be by at the time and offer them some advice—just when the previous stuffing has

brought, after the lapse of some time, its train of disease, since it was done without regard to what is wholesome—these are the people they will accuse and chide and harm as far as they can, while they will sing the praises of that former crew who caused the mischief. And you now, Callicles, are doing something very similar to this: you belaud men who have regaled the citizens with all the good cheer they desired. People do say they have made the city great; but that it is with the swelling of an imposthume, due to those men of the former time, this they do not perceive. For with no regard for temperance and justice they have stuffed the city with harbours and arsenals and walls and tribute and such-like trash; and so whenever that access of debility comes they will lay the blame on the advisers who are with them at the time, and belaud Themistocles and Cimon and Pericles, who caused all the trouble; and belike they will lay hold of you, if you are not on your guard, and my good friend Alcibiades, when they are losing what they had originally as well as what they have acquired, though you are not the authors, except perhaps part-authors, of the mischief. And yet there is a senseless thing which I see happening now, and hear of, in connexion with the men of former times. For I observe that whenever the state proceeds against one of her statesmen as a wrongdoer, they are indignant and protest loudly against such monstrous treatment: after all their long and valuable services to the state they are unjustly ruined at her hands, so they protest. But the whole thing is a lie; since there is not a single case in which a ruler of a city could ever be unjustly ruined by the very city that he rules. For it is very much the same with pretenders to statesmanship as with professors of sophistry. The sophists, in fact, with all their other accomplishments, act absurdly in one point: claiming to be teachers of virtue, they often accuse their pupils of doing them an injury by cheating them of their fees and otherwise showing no recognition of the good they have done them. Now what can be more unreasonable than this plea? That men, after they have been made good and just, after all their injustice has been rooted out by their teacher and replaced by justice, should be unjust through something that they have not! Does not this seem to you absurd, my dear friend? In truth you have forced me to make quite a harangue, Callicles, by refusing to answer.

CALL. And you are the man who could not speak unless somebody answered you?

SOC. Apparently I can. Just now, at any rate, I am rather extending my speeches, since you will not answer me. But in the name of friendship, my good fellow, tell me if you do not think it unreasonable for a man, while professing to have made another good, to blame him for being wicked in spite of having been made good by him and still being so?

CALL. Yes, I do.

JOHN LINTON MYRES (1868–1954) was chairman of the British School at Athens, president of the Hellenic Society, and honorary Fellow of both Magdalen and New College, Oxford. He was primarily associated with Oxford University, although he also taught at Liverpool, Manchester, and Cambridge and held the Sather Classical Professorship at the University of California. His books include *Who Were the Greeks?*, *Geographical History in Greek Lands*, *The Dawn of History*, and *Homer and His Critics*. What was it in the character of the Athenians themselves, he asks, that kept them from living up to the ideals of a potentially good state?*

► # *Where the Athenians Were Found Wanting*

The question has been often discussed how it came about that with political ideas so clearly and early defined, and such endowment of natural ability, the Greek people had a political history so checquered and disappointing, and in some respects even so futile. Looking back as he was already able to do, over the most brilliant period of political construction, Aristotle supplies, at all events, an outline of the answer. If men are to be good and useful individuals, and therewith good and useful members of a well-ordered state, three things are indispensable—breeding, training, reasoning.

Equality in Breed

By breeding he still means what the older aristocracies had so jealously maintained, purity and homogeneity of descent, as the best guarantee for sureness and uniformity of reaction to circumstances. Now, it was precisely this homogeneity which most Greek communities had lost, by Aristotle's time, through the relaxation of kinship-grouping, and the temptations of a "rich match" outside the circle of long-established corporator families. And of this modern promiscuity, Athens, the type-specimen of extreme democracy, was at the same time the conspicuous instance. . . . The

---

* From John L. Myres, *The Political Ideas of the Greeks*, (New York and Nashville: Abingdon Press, 1927), pp. 360–369. Reprinted by permission of Dr. J. N. L. Myres.

effects of the crossing of pure strains are already well known from experiments on many species of plants and animals. Among the "first-crosses" there are certain to be many individuals of unusual qualities and exceptional vigour, some reproducing characteristics of one of the parental strains, some those of the other. But there is no security that these "sports" will themselves breed true, however carefully mated with their like, and in the next generation, among the "second-crosses," there will no less certainly be a large proportion of individuals who are in every sense of the word "ill-bred"; of poor physique, incomposite, dysharmonic build, uncertain temper, and unstable character.

Now, this had been precisely the experience of Athens in the generations following the revolution of Cleisthenes. Down to this point in their history, with very few exceptions, such as the marriage of Megacles, son of Alcmaeon, with the heiress of the tyrant of Sicyon, not merely the Attic "nobility," but the population of every Attic *deme* had been of purely Attic descent for some five centuries. Then the bar to mixed marriages was abruptly removed; and in the generation which was growing up after the Persian Wars, there was an outbreak of exuberant energy in all ranks of life which has seldom been equalled, if ever. It was not only that in the positions of political initiative there were men like Cimon (who was partly Thracian, and not quite Greek either in appearance or in temperament), Thucydides, son of Melesias, and Pericles; it was the same among the potters, the sculptors, the bronze-workers, above all among the soldiers, seamen, and traders who made the reputation which the Athenians retained until the outbreak of the "great war" in 432. But in the course of that war we find Socrates raising the question whether human efficiency is hereditary, answering it in the negative, and illustrating his pessimism by the examples of those same men of exceptional ability, whose own children were of quite ordinary ability, if not even an anxiety to their friends. And here, too, what can only be described as a loss of "nerve" or "tone" was general. To the new shock of a general war the "second-cross" Athenians reacted quite otherwise than their grandfathers had done in the Persian crisis. Their tempers were uncertain, their judgment clouded by panic and prejudice, probably even their physique upset in a way that made them easier victims to war-crowding and insanitary surroundings than they might otherwise have been. Above all there was a notable lack of men of initiative and leadership, together with a superfluity of ill-balanced, temperamental enthusiasts, cranks, and wind-bags; the one really able man, Alcibiades, belonging to the same ancient and exceptionally original family which had thrown up Pericles among its own "second-crosses," and hereafter disappears from public life. What wonder if people began to take note of these signs of the times, and if Sparta was thought to owe much of its success in the great war to its abstention from that facile receptivity which had blotted the escutcheon of Athens.

Equality in Training

Aristotle's second requirement for good citizenship is training: and in this respect, too, the state which had been the pioneer in political experiment had been the victim of recurring accidents. For any public system of education family solidarity was still quite unprepared down to Socrates' time; Alcibiades' treatment of his teachers only put the fine point on the practical problem of moulding this human quicksilver at all; and the only contemporary sketch of a schoolmaster is the more eloquent because it is humour, not caricature. Consequently, such education as was possible was the business of the father and the boy's elder relatives, for the women, under the economic handicap of Greek society, could do little for him after the nursery stage. Even Alcestis, Euripides' ideal of what a Greek mother might be, worries herself but little about the future of her boy, though a good deal about the future of her girl. But three times during the fifth century Athens endured the ravages of a general war— against the Persians, against the League of the Land Powers from 460 to 445, and again against the World of Reaction after 432; not to mention the grave losses sustained by the way, between 476 and 460, in the "little wars" incidental to the reparation-period after the Persian retreat. Seldom, in the history of any community, has the young generation had to face its responsibilities earlier, or with less of that habitual, imperceptible, and most potent discipline of seeing "how father does it." Seldom, consequently, has there been greater need of some professional substitute for that home-training, or greater alacrity of response to the offers of foreign teachers, when they began to come. That the "sophistic" movement centred in Athens as it did is the clearest proof both of the severity of the strain on Athenian intellect and temper, imposed by those amazing experiences; and also of the "will-to-learn" exhibited by the young Athenian, and, on the whole, tolerated (and rightly) by his elders. What is instructive as well as pathetic about

Strepsiades in the *Clouds* of Aristophanes, is not that the old man knows nothing about education himself, either in theory, or to practise it, but that he is all too ready to register his son in the first "thinking-shop" he comes across, to make good his own omissions. Similarly, the whole plan of Plato's *Republic*, and still more of his *Laws*, presumes a general interest in educational problems among ordinary people, casually met, which has no parallel in literature until the Revival of Learning, and perhaps in our own time.

Equality in Intelligence

But both "breeding" and "training" are for Aristotle preliminaries only, in the creation of a good man and a good citizen. They are the conditions for that freedom and facility with which the mature "grown-up" individual is expected to use his own reason, both in personal and in public affairs. This rational intellectual ideal of citizenship is exemplified in the notable word regularly used to characterize the "desirable alien" whom a city-state from time to time "delighted to honour" by enrollment among the men of its own sort. Let breeding and training have been what fortune gave, what made a man acceptable for incorporation in a society so exclusive as every Greek city was in principle, was that he was "of a good intelligence toward us." Not sentimental loyalty, or physical heroism, or magnificent benevolence, but an honest, impartial man's application of hard commonsense, business acumen, "unforgetful" statesmanship, to the city's occasions and perplexities, was his title to this "order of merit."

Nor was this an easy task, for, as we have seen, the ideals of political "initiative" stood high. On the one hand there were the "ancestral customs" which had brought the city through great perils in the past, sometimes a "written" constitution, though the latest and completest example of a rechartered constitution shows how little of the "ancestral customs" it was thought necessary to rehearse in detail on such an occasion; sometimes a traditional code, precariously extorted as case-law from the "public servants" or the "council of elders," as the *themistes*[1] aforetime were "wrested" from the mind of Zeus. On the other was an ever-changing world of rival states and groupings of states, rival enterprises of individuals and associations of narrower scope than the state, and beyond all the Persian incubus, the Carthaginian incubus, in due time the Macedonian incubus, of which no one was qualified to say whether it was, as Isocrates[2] hoped, a revelation of the mind of Zeus for the undoing of Persia, or, as Demosthenes feared, a leviathan whose devastation of the Greek culture which the city-state had created and was maintaining, could be averted only, as Heraclitus had phrased it, by insistence on the custom of the city, as on the fortress wall, and yet more insistently.

Between those customs—different for each city, and rightly differing, as all agreed, because no two city-states were, or could be, quite the same—and these circumstances, no less differently affecting each several state, in its relation, for example, with the leviathan of the mo-

ment—adjustment was possible only by the exercise of that "good intelligence" which was so valued in the foreign benefactor, and so hard to ensure in the home-bred and home-trained. For it was precisely the revelation to this later phase of Hellenism, of that "gift of the Muses" which Hesiod had celebrated in the "salt of the earth," as he perceived them in the Early Iron Age. In the individual, both in his private affairs and in his discharge of public obligations, it is what is described uniformly as "reasonableness," or "equity," in the sense already described; as the will to take less, and give more, than the strict normal "way of doing things" presumed or required that you should. It was the quality most admired and valued, just because it was the hardest to exhibit, for people with the stern upbringing, intellectual alertness, and abounding vitality of the Greeks. It is the re-interpretation to a more ruthlessly rational age, of what *aidôs*[3] and *nemesis*[4] had expressed in days when the risk of disturbance was less from skill and subtlety than from exuberant "will-to-power." Pericles claimed this reasonableness as the characteristic of Athenians as he idealized them, believing democracy to be capable of this and predisposing men to it; and in the fourth century the opponents of democratic shifts and excesses claimed it for themselves, in mitigation, at all events, of the charge that because they made both ends meet in their own concerns they were "enemies of the people," who were taking such care that those ends should not overlap by much.

---

[1] These were the decrees of the gods.—*Ed.*

[2] One of the great teachers of rhetoric at Athens (his school opened in ca. 392 B.C.) ; the reference here is to the fact that he tried—or hoped—to convince Philip of Macedon to unite the Greek world peacefully and to march against Persia.—*Ed.*

[3] A very reverent sense of what the proper and decent man holds most dear.—*Ed.*

[4] Fate—in its retributive aspects.—*Ed.*

T. R. GLOVER (1869–1943) was professor of Latin
at Queens College, Ontario, and later university
lecturer in ancient history at St. John's, Cambridge.
His strong faith in the value of classical studies,
combined with his interest in literature and religion,
resulted in several beautifully written books:
*Life and Letters in the Fourth Century, The Conflict
of Religions in the Early Roman Empire, The
Jesus of History,* and *The Springs of Hellas.* If
the answer to the problem of decline is to be found
within the Athenians themselves, then, as Glover
asserts, in fairness to them we must not forget the
kind of responses that war evokes. His article
contains both his point of view and a sensitive
summary of the Athenians' "spiritual" failures.*

The Decline of Democracy

Every student of antiquity feels the
difference between the Greek world as
we know it in the fifth century B.C. and
as we find it in the two or three generations that follow the death of Socrates.
Whether we turn to historian or to
philosopher—for we shall hardly find
a poet—the impression is the same. Something has gone; the ideals are different;
men mistrust the future. Athens, Sparta
and Thebes have had their great days,
their span of rule; and, after all, the
real arbiter of Greece is the Persian
King. The last words of Xenophon's
history, the *Hellenica,* stay in our minds.
"After the battle (of Mantineia) con-
fusion and disorder were greater than

before in Greece. So far let my story go;
what follows shall perchance be another's
care." By 362 B.C. Xenophon was an old
man; he had seen one Greek power after
another fall; and no one knew what to
do; unless perhaps his old fellow-citizen,
Isocrates, were right and the future lay
neither with a democracy, nor with an
oligarchy, but with a king. Xenophon
drew the picture of a king in his *Agesi-
laos* as Isocrates had drawn another in
Evagoras; Greek both of them. And all
the time we, who look back on the story,
know that the future did lie with kings
and not with Greek kings. We are
warned by modern historians not to
think too gloomily of the fourth cen-

* From T. R. Glover, *Democracy in the Ancient World* (Cambridge, 1927), pp. 74–96. Reprinted by permission of the Cambridge University Press.

tury. Beloch will not allow us to believe it on Thucydides' word that the Peloponnesian War demoralized the Greeks; even in the early years of that war the historian tells us of facts that disprove it—"the war only unfettered the passions, which had slept during the preceding years of peace." Holm urges that the supposed degeneracy is not proved; there was, however, deviation from the old paths promoted by sophistry and rhetoric, but Democracy was not a factor of decay in Athens but rather a force for the moral preservation of the city.

It is worth while to turn back to the passage of Thucydides.

The whole Hellenic world was in commotion; in every city the chiefs of the democratic factions, and of the few, were struggling, the one to bring in the Athenians, the other the Lacedaemonians. Now in time of peace they would have had no excuse for introducing either and no desire to do so; but when they were at war and both sides could easily obtain allies, the dissatisfied parties were only too ready to invoke foreign aid. Revolution brought upon Hellas many terrible calamities, such as have been and always will be while human nature remains the same. In peace and prosperity both states and individuals are actuated by higher motives (or, conceivably, have better judgments) because they do not fall under the dominion of imperious necessities; but war takes away the comfortable provision of daily life, and is a violent teacher, and creates in most people a temper that matches their conditions.

In spite of Beloch's reminder of dark deeds done in the early years of war, it is hard not to feel that Thucydides is right. There is this, too, to remember, that Beloch and most of our scholars wrote before the European war of our own day. As one looks back upon that, the retrospect of Thucydides, returned from long exile, upon a Greece ruined by twenty-seven years of war, carries with it conviction. War is a violent schoolmaster, reckless and headlong, and gives his character to all his pupils, winners and losers. Shallow critics remark a certain cynicism in Thucydides, which I cannot accept. They might quote this passage with its sad hint that peace and prosperity affect our conduct and motives, but hardly change underlying character. Ancient historians say little of economic questions, but Thucydides glances here at an economic factor—the comfortable provision of daily life. We have seen, at least in Europe, what the disappearance of that involves. So human nature, stripped of the comforts of peace, breaks loose.

The cause of all these evils was the love of power originating in avarice and ambition, and the party-spirit engendered by them, when men are fairly engaged in a contest. For the leaders in the cities used specious names; some would plead political equality for the masses under the law, and the others the wisdom of an aristocracy. They committed the most monstrous crimes, yet even these were surpassed by the magnitude of their revenges; both alike made the caprice of the moment their law. . . . Thus revolution gave birth to every form of wickedness.

Human nature, war, passion, faction, and the daily food—all are militating against civil life. Of all forms of government, Democracy, as the speech of Pericles suggests, asks the most of its citizens; Democracy, least of all, can exist where passion, revenge, and hunger are making men reckless of everything that counts in civilization. Man ill-educated, says Plato, is the most savage of earthly creatures; and thirty years of war are not a good education.

War may be at least for one of the

parties to it inevitable. No sane person could apply that adjective to the Sicilian expedition voted in 416 by the Athenians. It was aggression; and, though Thucydides says that with wise leadership it could have been successful, it was folly. Mr. F. M. Cornford, in his brilliant book *Thucydides Mythistoricus*, advances a general theory of the historian and his work which I know of no one accepting; but he brings out most vividly certain things that we are apt to miss. Think of the phrases—"love sick with a fatal passion for what is out of reach," "few things are turned into success by desire," "a passion fell on all to sail forth . . . a longing for far-off sights and scenes," "a desire for more"; . . . this was the spirit in which the war was carried on and the fatal expedition was launched by Demos. The ancients have handed down to us the story of Assyria, ever desirous of more, a strong military power ambitious of dominating the whole earth, wrecked at last by years of attempting too much. We have read of the great reign of Louis XIV ending in loss and crippled strength as the result of the same ambition. We all think of another case. Every people realizes the folly of another people thinking it can indefinitely add province to province, find men and money to crush all resistance, and spread itself out so thin as to cover the globe, and yet escape the consequences of the weakness that follows over-straining of powers. Athenian Demos fell into the common temptation of Kings and Kaisers and financial oligarchs.

Before I began to write these lectures, two reflections were in my mind as I thought of Athens and other democracies. Nations break down abroad, but they are ruined at home. It is foreign policy that finds out the weakness of our theories. Aristotle criticizes the political ideas of Phaleas of Chalcedon—his institutions "are chiefly designed to promote the internal welfare of the state; but the legislator should consider also its relation to neighbouring nations and to all who are outside of it." Phaleas had much to say about equality of property when he sketched his ideal; he expected it to "take away from a man the temptation to be a highwayman because he is hungry or cold." Hunger and cold we all understand more or less; if those were the only problems of government, we might have found Aristotle less uncongenial to us in his discussion of the artisan as citizen. But he lays his finger on the spot; Utopias are wrecked on foreign policy. It is very hard to understand this, and what is equally true—that in the long run every problem is linked up with foreign policy, in a world where every conceivable state has frontiers and neighbours beyond them, and where as to-day nobody is far away. But a breakdown in foreign policy betrays weakness at home—some failure to realize and to understand, some defect in training or temper, something intellectually or morally wrong, undeveloped or perverted.

The failure of the Sicilian expedition brought the Persian once more on to the Mediterranean. He had been kept off the seas, as we saw, by the Athenian fleet, and now Athens ruled the seas no more, and he returned to play one Greek power off against another. We need not follow events in any detail. It was Persian subsidies and ships that at last gave Sparta her victory in 404; it was Persian money and a Persian victory that restored the walls of Athens in 393. Six years later the King's Peace made it plain to everybody who it was that controlled, if he did not rule, every Greek city around the Aegean. The old antithesis of 479 still held; whatever hopes Greek oligarchs or democrats might cherish of a city of their own, governed by themselves, of being *autopolitan,* no city was or could be isolated, every city must look to the hegemony, the suzerainty, of some Greek power or the undisguised rule of Persia. They had tried a democratic suzerainty, and it broke down; Sparta's attempt was far more helpless and hopeless from the start; so, failing Athens, Persia was in control—a monarchic power over oligarchies and democracies alike.

The Greek republic had broken down all round. Greek war was always savage, . . . and Greek faction was, if anything, more savage still. Broadly, in the two hundred and fifty cities in the Athenian confederacy, there was for the seventy years of its duration little revolution. There were revolts, as we know, but the Athenian maintenance of democracies left revolution little chance. The war, as Thucydides tells us, and especially the fall of Athens, gave faction its opportunity. We read of revolution in the cities before the Persian War; the story goes on after the fall of Athens, all through the fourth century, and Polybius in the second century lets us see the grim old business still in process— the war of faction and neighbour—till Rome took away all their liberties, and ended their wars for ever in "the boundless majesty of Roman peace." If it can be urged that the wars and factions of the early Greek states contributed something to the Greek spirit and really helped to develop Greek genius, it cannot be said of them after the fall of Athens. From then onwards they meant

less and less, and did nothing but weaken and dispirit the Greek people. No wonder the old centres of Greek life were gradually depopulated; no wonder men of spirit threw over the wretched little city-state for careers of sense and peace in the new foundations of the kings eastward and the manifold life without politics of the growing Roman world westward.

We know from our own experience how war dislocates trade and ruins industry. So we say, in our abstract style. What it really does is to destroy property, to divert men from useful employment, to pervert the spirit of enterprise. When peace at last returned to the Greek world on the victory of Sparta, there had been twenty-seven years of war. In a striking passage Isocrates sums up what the wars of Athenian imperialists had cost—

they met with more and greater disasters in the period of empire than ever befell the city in all time. To Egypt sailed two hundred triremes and were lost with all their crews, round Cyprus one hundred and fifty. In Datum they lost ten thousand hoplites of their own and their allies, in Sicily forty thousand men and two hundred and forty triremes, and finally on the Hellespont two hundred triremes. Incidental losses of ten, or five, or more triremes, and of men one or two thousand at a time, who could number?

Old families, he adds, were extinguished and their places taken by foreigners. Even if antipathy to imperialist ambitions leads Isocrates to some heightening of phrase, it is plain that in ships and men Athens lost terribly; and all the time war and the necessity of building warships turned the dockyards from the production of merchantmen. It is true

hat Athens' geographical position in
he centre of the Greek world, her harbours and the conservatism of commerce
gave her back a fair measure of prosper-
ty far more quickly than could have
been expected. Ships had to take goods
for exchange to some emporium, and
they went to the Peiraieus once more
and were welcome.

But the effects of war upon industry
are manifold and intricate. . . . The
crew of a warship was presumably larger
than that of a . . . merchant ship. What
became of the men who manned the
navy during the eleven years following
the battle of Aegospotami, we can only
conjecture. That the Spartans killed a
lot of them or left them to drown is not
a malignant guess from Spartan character. They very possibly sold others into
slavery, as they did some of Xenophon's
Ten Thousand. Many must have dis-
persed, and quite probably many Athenian sailors were on the Persian fleet
which won the battle of Cnidos in 394,
the victory which led to the rebuilding
of the walls. General shipping, if we
may judge from the speeches that survive from law trials of a half century,
gradually revived and would absorb
some of the men from the old war-fleets.
With the armies of Greece it was
different. . . . The war lasted off and
on twenty-seven years; and from what
we have seen in our own time, the
training, we may guess, was more intense and developed as the years dragged
on. The forces of all the states concerned
had in most cases abruptly to adjust
themselves to peace, without preparation
trained soldiers, untrained in agriculture or industry; and they had nothing
to do. Their one trade of fighting was
in theory not required, but they had no
other; they were bound to be soldiers

somewhere or other, wherever they could
find pay.

The mercenary soldier is then a permanent and an outstanding figure in the
fourth century. Soldiering becomes a
trade, first because old soldiers had no
other, and gradually because supply can
create demand. . . . So the profession
of mercenary soldier flourished till the
Roman imposed peace. . . .

The devastation of Greece helped to
turn men away from the land to the
wandering life of the mercenary. . . . In
Attica ten years of enemy occupation
had ruined agriculture. Now it is true,
as Adam Smith drily said, when he was
told in 1777 that England was ruined,
that "there is a lot of ruin in a nation."
For two centuries [the farmer's staple]
had been more and more the olive and
the vine; and an olive tree takes some
eighteen years to reach its best fertility.
The farm people had had to live in the
city, as best they could, and do other
things. No doubt a proportion of them
gradually got back to the land and the
old life. But we learned from Aristotle
that a change in the proportions of the
state affects its character, and the war
made that change in Athens. If the
farmers are, as Aristotle said, the best
and safest element in the state, then the
result of the war and its changes will be
a worse democracy.

Industry also had suffered. Athens
from Solon's day onward had been one
of the great manufacturing centres, probably the greatest, of Greece. She had
come to depend more with time on slave
labour, not wholly but largely, and,
"more than twenty thousand slaves had
run away, a large proportion of them
artisans. . . ." A story is told, by Xenophon, about a man with fourteen refugee
women relatives in his house, all idle

and quarrelsome; and how Socrates suggested to him to set them weaving, and so to silence their tongues and fill their mouths; and how successful the experiment was. Years after this—half a century later—in 355 B.C., Isocrates says the great problem in Athens is want; with the larger part of the people the chief interest in life is how to live *this* day. To keep the democracy going at all, payment had to be made for attendance not merely in the Law Courts but in the sovereign Ecclesia itself. Payment of representatives is called a modern democratic device; here it was paying the People itself to rule.

I have already hinted however that in one phase of life Athens recovered surprisingly quickly. She had been and she remained what the Greeks called the [*emporium*] of Greece—the centre of business and the centre of distribution. . . . The harbours of Athens remained, and the tradition; and Athenians were quick to see the value of it. As a pamphleteer of our period says, everything attracted commerce to the Peiraieus; you can unload your ship quickly, very quickly and without delay or demurrage get a new freight; or if you perfer you can take silver, with the sure knowledge that Athenian drachmas, with the familiar owl on them, are everywhere accepted at par. If agriculture and industry were crippled, there was more and more work around the docks, loading and unloading, ship-building and repairing—another emphasis on one particular section of the population with obvious results. Ship-building may under good conditions be a more or less stable trade; ship-repairing, loading and unloading evidently depend on seasons and on weather. A spell of bad weather will stop work; a sudden return of fair winds fills the harbour with ships running in that were held up, and there is a wild demand for labour. I always feel that moderns, who echo too faithfully the complaints of Demosthenes that Athenians would not undertake military training and military service, forget the docks and the weather, and only imperfectly realize that Commerce will not wait about for drill-sergeants. . . .

Let us try to sum up what we have reached as regards Athens; and let us remember that Athens was not all Greece, but that, in spite of Sparta, and with proper reservations, we may take the general experience of Athens as illustrative of the rest of Greece. The fourth century shows us a crippled people, suffering from all the losses of life and property that a long and savage war had brought, and from all the less traceable but not less real losses, that follow disappointment and the belief that energy and effort will be more or less futile. The old, old handicap of Greece is still there—every city must be absolutely independent of every other city . . . Internationally Democracy has failed. The thoroughgoing democrat like the true Utopian he is, has forgotten the world outside. The prime business of every government is "a full dinner pail," if I may borrow a modern politician's "slogan." Where and how are you to fill it for a dockyard population, dependent on the ships of foreigners who use your *emporion*, when most of the wheat that you or your fathers have eaten for two centuries comes hundreds of miles from Southern Russia? That is the business of the state.

The full dinner pail? It was pretty empty by now. Let me quote to you an episode alleged to have taken place in the assembly. I think it probably did not strictly take place at all, that it is mere parody; but the merest parody must parody something. Let us hear Aristophanes first, however, and afterwards decide whether to believe him.[1]

Chremes:

Next came Evaeon, smart accomplished chap,
Stark-naked as the most of us supposed,
But he himself insisted he was clothed.
He made a popular democratic speech;
Behold, says he, *I am myself in want
Of cash to save me; yet I know the way
To save the citizens and save the State.
Let every clothier give to all who ask
Warm woolen robes, when first the sun
     turns back;
No more will pleurisy attack us then.
Let such as own no bed-clothes and no bed
After they've dined, seek out the furriers,
     there
To sleep; and whoso shuts the door against
     them
In wintry weather, shall be fined three
     blankets.*

Blepyros:

Well said indeed; and never a man would
     dare
To vote against him had he added this:
*That all who deal in grain shall freely give
Three quarts to every pauper or be hanged.*

Chremes continues with more amazing news; the assembly has actually voted that the whole State be handed over to be ruled by the women. It is surprising, but quoth the good Chremes,

                    Well, if it be
For the State's good, we needs must all obey.
There is a saying of the olden time,
That all the vain and silly things we vote,
All of them, somehow work the public good.
So be it now, high Pallas and ye gods!

[1] Aristophanes, *Ecclesiazusae*, 408ff. The rendering is mostly that of Mr. B. B. Rogers.

Chremes is a good democrat, with the good democrat's invincible faith that it all comes out all right. I have read something very like it—very like it, indeed—in Lord Bryce's *American Commonwealth*, in a chapter entitled "The Fatalism of the Multitude," where he shows how in a more modern democracy the loyal citizen believes the majority is sure to go right and that it is his part to fall in, whatever his own private judgment might have been.

The immediate consequence, Aristophanes tells us, of feminine government is a thoroughgoing system of state socialism.

The rule which I dare to enact and declare
Is that all shall be equal and equally share
All wealth and enjoyments, nor longer endure
That one should be rich and another be
     poor.

This equality is to cover slaves, silver, land, food, clothing, wine and peanuts; and sex, especially sex—absolute equality and complete control by law in sexual relations as well as in land tenure and precious metals.

No, it was never really carried out; it was all mockery, parody, playfulness—the genius of Aristophanes. But two odd things, or three, may be noted. Socialist ideas were obviously in the air, or they could not be parodied, and they were the outcome of very general poverty. Next, *after* Aristophanes had produced his play, Plato published his *Republic*, where a great many of the things at which Aristophanes laughed are seriously discussed. . . . The third thing to note is how modern it all seems and how much less like parody since the war. And a fourth thing would be the reflection that it all amounts to a confession that Democracy has failed. It failed in the war, it now fails in peace.

If you object that I am treating Comedy too seriously, I deny it outright; but, not to bicker, I will turn to Aristotle again, who is not a comic poet nor an idealist like Plato, and he shall tell us again what people were actually doing. Men readily listen to that sort of idealist talk, he says, and "are easily induced to believe that in some wonderful manner everybody will become everybody's friend, especially when someone is heard denouncing the evils now existing in states, suits about contracts, convictions for perjury, flatteries of rich men and the like, which are said to arise out of the possession of private property." We have heard it, too, this tracing of all sin to private property—but, says Aristotle, the true cause lies elsewhere, in the wickedness of human nature. Ruined fortunes and revolution go together, he says, but to have equality of fortunes (which contributes to peace) the legislator must fix the number of the children.

If the poor, because they are more in number, divide among themselves the property of the rich, is not this unjust? No, by heaven (will be the reply), for the lawful authority willed it. Again, when all has been taken, and the majority divide anew the property of the minority, is it not evident, if this goes on, that they will ruin the State?

So it looks as if re-division of property was discussed. But the actual procedure was along lines of less challenge and more security. The demagogues lay information against individual rich men, diminish their property by imposition of public services and prosecute them

with a view to the confiscation of their wealth. They often get property confiscated in the law courts in order to please the people. In the last and worst form of Democracy the citizens are very numerous and can hardly be made to assemble unless they are paid, and to pay them, when there are no revenues, presses hardly upon the notables—for the money must be obtained by a property tax and confiscations and corrupt practices of the law courts. These deliberate manoeuvres to despoil the rich in contempt of justice in order to give demagogic largess to the many are attested by Isocrates.

We have, no doubt, always to qualify the laments of man as to contemporary degeneration. It may be argued, with facts to support the thesis, that fourth-century Athens was not such a bad place, that it became the centre of what might be left of Greek genius, the hearth and home of Greek philosophy. Old men are not always fair to their juniors, as their juniors are not to them, and Isocrates lived to an immense age. But picture a society where the following sentence is possible in a law court: "You must reflect that you have often heard these men tell you that, if you do not condemn whom they bid you condemn, there will be no state pay for you." It comes to us confirmed all round —Aristotle was not, perhaps, thinking specially of Athens, nor was Polybius, whose retrospect on Greek democracy may suffice for this phase of our subject. He sums up in several chapters his reflections on the variety of Greek governments as a prelude to his great account of Rome's distinguishing features. He chronicles the decline of Greek Democracy, the last days of which he had seen, and he remembers many Greek states in Greece itself and in Sicily.

When a new generation arises and the democracy falls into the hands of children's children, they have become so accustomed to freedom and equality that they no longer value them, and begin to aim at pre-eminence; and it is chiefly those of ample fortune who fall into this error . . . and they ruin their estates; tempting and corrupting the common people in every way. And hence, when once by their foolish thirst for reputation they have made the many ready and greedy for bribes, then democracy in its turn is abolished and changes into a government of violence and the fist. . . . For the mob, accustomed to feed at the expense of others and to have its hopes of a livelihood in the property of its neighbours, as soon as they find a leader who is ambitious and daring but is excluded from the honours of office by poverty, perfects the rule of the fist, and uniting its forces sets in motion massacres, banishments, redivisions of the land, till, fully brutalized, it finds again a master and monarch. This is the cycle of constitutional change, the economy of Nature.

Herodotus long before had lingered over the beautiful word, the most beautiful of words, [*isonomia*], equality before the law. But equality was an idea that men carried further, and it became ambiguous. In the old days, says Isocrates, they did not mean by Democracy mere want of self-control . . . , by freedom abuse of law, by equality before the law (the word of Herodotus) recklessness. There were in fact two *equalities*, one which gave the same to all, while the other gave what was fitting to each group. They did not elect their officers by lot but chose the best man. Which all seems very like ordinary Toryism, no doubt, and Isocrates was

already seventy-five. Some people, says Aristotle, argue that those who are by nature equals must have the same right and worth, and that for unequals to have an equal share, or for equals to have an unequal share, in the offices of state, is as bad as for different bodily constitutions to have the same food and clothing, or the same different. But, as he says, "granted that equals ought to have equality, there still remains a question—equality or inequality of what? Here is a difficulty which the political philosopher has to resolve." But it was Greek observation that demagogues were not political philosophers, they were practical men, flatterers of the *demos*. Hence "it has now become a habit among the citizens of states not even to care about equality";

and in democracies of the more extreme type there has arisen a false idea of freedom which is contradictory to the true interests of the state. For two principles are characteristic of Democracy, the government of the majority and freedom. Men think that what is just is equal; and that equality is the supremacy of the popular will and that freedom and equality mean doing what a man likes. In such democracies everyone lives as he pleases. . . .

And elsewhere Aristotle recurs to this—

Every citizen, it is said, must have equality, and therefore in a democracy the poor have more power than the rich, because there are more of them and the will of the majority is supreme. This, then, is one note of liberty which all democrats affirm to be the principle of their state. Another is that a man should live as he likes. . . . This, they say, is the privilege of a freeman; and, on the other hand, not to live as a man likes is the mark of a slave. This is the second characteristic of Democracy, whence has arisen the claim of men to be ruled by none if possible, or, if this is impossible, to rule and be ruled in turns.

Every kind of constitution, says Polybius, is exposed by nature to some form of degeneration, and the danger of Democracy is to decline into the animals' way of life, sheer brute force. They get into their heads a wrong definition of freedom, says Aristotle.

Let us try again, and see what Plato says. Plato came of a family critical of Democracy; he saw Democracy go under in the war with a state founded on principle; and Demos made Socrates drink the hemlock. But Plato was great enough to see both sides of an issue and to recognize that old Demos has his points. Still his picture is grim. Democracy comes into being after the poor have conquered their opponents, slaughtering some and banishing some, while to the remainder they give an equal share of freedom and power. And their manner of life? In the first place, are they not free; and is not the city full of freedom and frankness—a man may say and do what he likes? There is much merit in a question. Isocrates bluntly wrote that there is *no* freedom of speech in a democracy— . . . "all along it has been your custom to expel everybody who did not advocate your pleasures." Plato follows up his question with another—then in this kind of state will there not be the greatest variety of human natures? Then it seems likely to be the fairest of states, like an embroidered robe spangled with every kind of flower—a sort of bazar where you can pick what you want, a whole assortment of constitutions, all because of the liberty there. And any man can do as he likes—hold office or avoid it, go to war

or remain at peace, whatever others do. See, too, the forgiving spirit of Democracy and the "don't care" about trifles— her indifference to the training of citizens, her satisfaction in anybody who claims to be the people's friend! 'Tis a sweet form of government, anarchic, anything, with equality alike for equal and unequal.

From this Plato passes on to his famous description of the democratic man. He, too, is a democracy in himself —his mind is a democracy of inclinations, full of vain conceits that teach him to call modesty silliness, and temperance unmanliness, and send them packing; and, when they have swept his soul clean of them, they bring into him insolence and anarchy and waste and impudence in bright array with garlands on their heads; and he lives as he likes. One desire is as good as another, all alike; and he lives from day to day indulging the fancy of the hour, everything by turns and spasms, whatever comes into his head; his life has neither law nor order, and he answers to the state that produces him. "This absence of principle he, like the democratic state, makes into a principle." He lives as he likes. And, if we count all this again parody, let us recall the Cynic movement in Philosophy and the schools that followed—Stoic and Epicurean and Sceptic,—for all of whom the unit was the individual and not the state. Diogenes was not Plato's democratic man; he had a central idea, an idea negative of human experience, of human society, of mankind; he would live like a dog.

Let us again sum up what we have gathered. The rule of the majority was the thing—of the untutored multitude, democratic men with no clear grasp of principle but possessed of a strong sense of the advantages of living as one likes, and holding in lieu of principle the belief that the majority can do no wrong, that everything comes right. Contemporary education reinforced the plain man in all this, or Plato would never have spent forty years in writing books against sophists and rhetoricians. But there they were, preaching Nature against law or convention, and emphasizing the individual. Small wonder if the individual accepted a gospel or a philosophy that squared so well with his natural instincts, his appetites and prejudices. Justice was the interest of the stronger. The common man chose to ignore the obvious fact that this justified every tyrant that extinguished liberty; he chose to take it as giving him his charter. The Confederacy, formed to protect all Greeks against the Persians, the Athenian turned into an Empire for himself; and, as he carried on his industries with slave labour, he made his allies support the Athenian *demos*. He limited admission to Athenian citizenship—Pericles himself did this or accepted it. He plumed himself on his city being an education to Greece, and turned it into "a co-operative society for making dividends for the citizens." He remodelled law to suit his mood. He cut himself adrift from the facts of the outside world,—Demos and Napoleon both did it, and each paid for the awful mistake. He made a sort of Utopia of his Athens and broke down on foreign policy. The Persian found the Greeks for the moment standing unsteadily side by side; he bungled his campaign, and Greeks were free never to unite in any real spirit again, and they succumbed one by one to another Prince of less power but more judgment. Greeks talked incessantly of equality and butchered one another like French revolutionists to get it; of freedom, and lived on the labour of slaves and allies. Individualism, particularism—how shall we put it? want of outlook, *Hybris*, no sense of self-restraint, what shall we say? We may find ourselves using the language of Greek drama or of the Gospels before we are done. Greek Democracy fell for want of foreign policy, for want of intelligence of outsider and neighbour, for want of that great and peculiarly Greek gift of *aidos*, the thought of the feelings and claims and rights of other men.

And yet, when all is said, it was Greek Democracy that gave us the standards by which we measure its failures—that gave us the ideas of law and self-government, of equality and liberty—that showed us what power is given to man, his mind and spirit—that taught us to face the universe and grasp it as a whole —that taught us the meaning of beauty and created it in its most imperishable forms—that gave us the spirit of self-criticism. Democracy is the form of government that asks the most of every citizen; the Greeks taught us that lesson in all their triumphs, and the same lesson is to read again, it is confirmed, in their failure to achieve and to maintain the ideals they saw.

ROBERT M. MacIVER (1882–   ), taught
at the University of Aberdeen, Scotland, at the
University of Toronto, and was Lieber
Professor of Political Philosophy and Sociology at
Columbia University when he retired from teaching
in 1950. His sociological perspective leads him to
see the foundations of political forms in the minds
of the people as well as in social institutions. Using
Athenian democracy as an example, in the selection
that follows he analyzes democratic government
as an experiment that evolves in conjunction with
the development of the ideas of democracy among
the body politic and the emergence of social
mechanisms for making it work. Democracy,
he believes, need not be thought of in terms of
success or failure, but rather in terms of the stages
in its development, and the conditions under which it
flourishes.*

The Ways of Democracy

Democracy is a form of government that is never completely achieved. This condition makes it harder to identify and harder to assess than oligarchy. Oligarchy presents no problem of definition, but there is much dispute over the definition of democracy. Democracy grows into its being. There may be centuries of growth before we can say: "Now this state is a democracy." Democracy must be prepared for in a manner that has no precedent in oligarchical systems. A sheer oligarchy can scarcely become all at once a democracy, however much its institutions may be revolutionized. But a democracy can be overthrown and turned into an oligarchy in the very moment of a *coup d'état*. All the characteristic systems of democracy that the world has seen have evolved through processes in which the instruments of government have gradually been brought under the control of the body of citizens as a whole. Where revolutions have occurred their violent impact has meant the sudden overthrow of an established oligarchy rather than the sudden creation of an effective democracy. The French Revolution proclaimed with the destruction of the *ancien régime* the inauguration of a most unqualified democracy. But the French people had to

* Reprinted with the permission of The Macmillan Company from *The Web of Government* by Robert M. MacIver. Copyright 1947 by Robert M. MacIver.

pass thereafter through many trials and conflicts before any kind of working democracy was attained.

In a democracy the people control. But who are the people and how do they control? Let us turn to the first great experiment in democratic government, that of Athens. It culminated in the time of Pericles, and we have seen how un-grudgingly it bestowed on the citizens the control over all their affairs. But it lasted a very short time, through part of the fifth century B.C., and though there were brief and partial revivals of democracy in the century that followed we cannot read the story without per-ceiving on what insecure foundations the democratic structure was built. After all, as we can learn from their litera-ture, the *myth* of democracy did not bite deep into the minds of this people. They had, in their various groups, conceived a fine passion for liberty, but they had little care for the conditions of liberty. There was not enough sense of the com-mon to sustain the common weal against. the fierce conflicts of interests and fac-tions. The great political philosophers were hostile to democracy. The sophists mockingly dissected it. The great trage-dians were interested in the aristocratic legends. The great comedian, Aristoph-anes, ridiculed it, and made open sport of the one poet who was democrati-cally minded, Euripides, and the one thinker who seemed to find it congenial, Socrates. The people were so little con-scious of their own champions that they banished Euripides—the not too moral Athenians condemned him for immoral sentiments—and put Socrates to death. The spirit of democracy did not pervade the form. The most powerful clubs in Athens were frankly oligarchical.

It is true that the intrusion of external powers into Athenian affairs would in any event have rendered the mainte-nance of democracy difficult, but this situation was in large measure due to the lack of any national spirit in Greece. Without the spirit of nationalism, or at least without the recognition of the unity of a people, it is hard to lay a sure foundation of democracy. The Greeks were highly conscious of their cultural difference from other peoples, but cultural attainment varies for in-dividuals and groups. It is a matter of degree, and each Greek city was very conscious of the difference between its culture and that of its neighbors and rivals. In his memorable Funeral Speech Pericles is almost wholly concerned with the great cultural qualities displayed by Athens, but that culture flowered only in a small circle of the people of Athens. It varied with opportunity and position and wealth and upbringing. Nationality has no degrees. It is equal in the least and in the greatest. Therefore it makes the people one in a way that neither the. finest nor the most pervasive culture can ever by itself assure.

So to the question: "Who are the people?" Athenian democracy gave a restrictive answer. The people were the citizens. So far as the citizens were con-cerned democracy, while it lasted, was remarkably thoroughgoing. The last stronghold of oligarchy, the control of justice, had fallen into their hands. Large popular courts, the members of which were drawn by lot from the en-rolled citizens, rendered the verdict in the great majority of cases. Every voter, through a system of rotation and of lot, had the opportunity to be magistrate, judge, or other official. The plebeian farmer or lamp-maker could rise to the highest power and defeat the great landowner or the renowned patrician. On all political issues the citizens freely decided in their assembly. But the citizens were a smallish fraction of the population of Attica, the territory of the Athenian State.

No more could be expected, given the conditions. The degree of democracy attained by Athens exceeded by far anything that the most forward visionary could have dreamed in advance. Such as it was, it created serious dangers to the state, for the people were still untutored in the ways of democracy and they banished or condemned to death some of their greatest men. They sent Aristides "the just" and their great leader Themistocles into exile, and they broke the influence of Pericles by bringing his famous Aspasia to trial for "impiety." Leadership was a dangerous profession in Athens. We can scarcely then be surprised that the citizens constituted in effect a privileged class. The citizen roll was jealously guarded and only the sons of free Athenian parents were admitted. The outlying population of Attica, for the most part illiterate, could hardly leave the soil and take on the duties or exercise the rights of citizens. Resident aliens were debarred from citizenship. And below them were the slaves, constituting more than a third of the population, who had no rights whatever. As for women, they were still kept—all except the high-class *hetairai* or courtesans—in a kind of Oriental seclusion. Thus the limited democracy of Athens had an anti-democractic base. While this situation prevailed the principle of democracy could never find its true expression or its true justification.

Similar conditions limited and finally defeated the Roman experiment in democracy. As Rome grew to power its economy came to depend more and more on a slave basis. The institution of slavery, not only in Rome but everywhere in the ancient world, presented an insuperable bar to the realization of democracy. For democracy vindicates the rights of the person apart altogether from his social status and the status of slave meant a total rejection of the person as bearer of civil rights. This denial, so long as the institution was accepted, precluded altogether any true conception of democracy. Slavery, being so universal, was taken to be a permanent condition of human society. Men found it hard to think in any other terms. The great thinkers of Greece had come to terms with the institution. Plato regarded a servile class as being in the nature of things and Aristotle made an elaborate defense of the institution, declaring that the slave was an animate tool, a body fitted to be an instrument, designed by nature for this service. Both philosophers fell into inconsistency and revealed the speciousness of their argument when they said that only foreigners should be slaves, never Greeks. But in an age before the advent of machine power there seemed to be no way around the difficulty that the heavy toil of the field and the mine and the workshop required the devotion of many men to servile tasks, if other men were to be free to build a higher civilization. So the philosophers, like other men, adjusted their doctrines to the conditions. Only an occasional free lance "sophist" or a rebel like the poet Euripides had anything to say against it. We should observe, however, that in the later days of Rome a more democratic spirit began to prevail among the leaders of thought. Cicero rejects the doctrine of the inherent inequality of peoples or classes.

Seneca refutes the idea that any men are by nature slaves. The Stoics laid stress on the universal reason that moved in human beings, and, like St. Paul, made no difference between "bond" and "free." The Roman jurists, accepting the fact of slavery, nevertheless came to contrast the civil inequality that separates the slave from the freeman with the equality that belonged to all men under the law of nature. Thus the intellectual foundations of democracy were being prepared.

The fact of slavery encouraged the tendency to regard all who engaged in menial toil or in the humbler forms of economic enterprise as an inferior order of human beings unworthy of civil rights. We must remember that not only in the ancient world but everywhere on the face of the earth at all earlier times —and it is still true over very large areas —the vast majority was uneducated, uncared for, uncouth, living rudely without resources, without communications, without opportunities of any kind. The idea of inclusive democracy was thereby checked. It seemed to have no relevance to the life of the peasant, and the peasants far outnumbered the rest of the population. Democracy, where it appeared, was a phenomenon of the city, of the privileged body of men who had escaped from the common lot. The city (*polis*) was the state, the rest of the country was its hinterland, the territory it owned. Democracy was the prerogative of citizens—and citizens were still city-dwellers. This conception had its most remarkable application in the later Roman Republic, which granted its citizenship throughout its far-extending dominions. But citizenship was still the right of membership within the city of Rome, and the gift of it to the world without made it more an honorary badge than a civil function. Only at a much later time, when the idea of nationalism grew strong, was the concept of citizenship given its full democratic significance. It is interesting that the principle of representation, the only method by which a country could be democratically governed, was practically unknown in the ancient world.

These considerations explain why democracy had so narrow a range in Athens and in Rome and why it was not strong enough to resist the tides of change. Not one alone, but several of the necessary conditions of a state-wide democracy were lacking. We may summarize the unfavorable conditions as being:

(1) the servile basis of ancient economies;

(2) the effectual limitation of cultural opportunities to relatively small privileged classes;

(3) the absence of the conception of nationality;

(4) the concomitant lack of any developed doctrine of democracy, resting on the political rights of persons as persons.

Suggestions for Further Reading

The scope of this bibliography is broader than the topic of the failure of Athenian democracy. No list of pertinent books would be complete which did not include some works on the general nature and problems of the city-state in classical Greece. Of these, one of the best introductions to the concept and meaning of the Athenian *polis*, and particularly to the economic problems that led to the decline of the political ideal, is still Alfred E. Zimmern, *The Greek Commonwealth: Politics and Economics in Fifth Century Athens* (London, 1911), now available as Oxford Paperback 13 (1961). Victor Ehrenberg, *The Greek State* (Oxford, 1960) —and Norton paperback N250—contains an excellent discussion of the origins and nature of the *polis*, a brief but penetrating analysis of the Athenian failure, and an up-to-date bibliography. W. W. Fowler, *The City-State of the Greeks and Romans*, first published in 1893 and reprinted recently (London, 1960), is an interpretative political history which is pertinent and useful. Although he tends to excuse slavery and the empire, Fowler emphasizes the fact that when the *polis* became imperial, it ceased to be a *polis* in the true definition of that term, and achieved a new kind of political structure that threatened the city-states throughout the Greek world.

The establishment and operation of the democracy is discussed, although usually only briefly, in most of the standard histories of Greece. The first four essays in *The Greek Political Experience: Studies in Honor of William Kelly Prentice*, edited by A. C. Johnson (Princeton, N.J., 1941) provide good historical background by eminent scholars on the transition to democracy at Athens, the democracy itself, and Athens and the League which grew into an empire. J. A. O. Larsen, "Cleisthenes and the Development of the Theory of Democracy at Athens," in *Essays in Political Theory Presented to George H. Sabine*, edited by Milton R. Konvitz and Arthur E. Murphy (Ithaca, N.Y., 1948) 1–16, and Victor Ehrenberg, "Origins of Democracy," *Historia, 1* (1950), 515–548, both treat the emergence of democracy and the earliest meanings given to the term.

For detailed studies of the constitution itself, James Day and Mortimer Chambers, *Aristotle's History of Athenian Democracy* (Berkeley, Calif., 1962), Robert J. Bonner, *Aspects of Athenian Democracy* (Berkeley, Calif., 1933), and C. Hignett, *A History of the Athenian Constitution to the End of the Fifth Century* B.C. (Oxford, 1952) are particularly valuable. In the last of these, Hignett argues that the rise of the demagogues aggravated the problems Athens faced at home (party conflicts) and abroad (the Peloponnesian War) and he therefore stresses as a major factor in the decline the "divorce between influence and responsibility." There are also individual studies on some of the features which were peculiar to Athenian democracy and which are relevant to the issues raised in the readings on the actual operation of the constitution. These include Robert J. Bonner and Gertrude Smith, *The Administration of Justice from Homer to Aristotle*, 2 vols., (Chicago, 1930); Jérôme Carcopino, *L'ostracisme athénien* (Paris, 1935), and J. W. Headlam, *Election by Lot at Athens*, 2d edition revised by D. C. Macgregor (Cambridge, 1933).

Herbert J. Muller, in *Freedom in the Ancient World* (New York, 1961), enlarges on many of the ideas discussed in the excerpt from *The Uses of the Past* and, with other additions, on the point that the Athenian democratic constitution did not provide for a loyal opposition, did not protect the rights of the minority, that in fact and in spirit it lacked a bill of rights.

The Greek theory of democracy must be pieced together from a variety of sources—plays, history, philosophy, orations. Donald Kagan has done this in two books that should be read simultaneously. In *The Great Dialogue: History of Greek Political Thought from Homer to Polybius* (New York, 1965) he discusses the democratic political theory in Chapter Five; in *Sources in Greek Political Thought* (New York, 1965) he presents the major ancient authors in translation (also Chapter Five).

An admirable work of scholarship has recently been produced on the ancient texts relating to the tribute imposed by Athens on her imperial colonies. The third volume of *The Athenian Tribute Lists*, by Benjamin D. Meritt, H. T. Wade-Gery, and Malcolm F. McGregor (Princeton, N.J., 1950), contains a summary of the evidence provided by the texts, which supports the position that Athens was parasitic on the empire; the fourth volume (1953) contains a long bibliography on the complex relationships between Athens and the empire.

Moses I. Finley has drawn together some of the leading arguments—all previously published—dealing with many aspects of the problem of slavery in *Slavery in Classical Antiquity: Views and Controversies* (Cambridge, England, 1960). The Marxist view that Athenian democracy declined essentially and inevitably because of the class conflict between slave-owners and slaves is amplified by the socialist historian George Thomson in *Studies in Greek Society*, vol. II (London, 1955). It does not seem likely that the controversy will end, and Chester G. Starr believes that modern scholars tend to misinterpret the entire pattern of ancient slavery

—what he has called "An Overdose of Slavery," *Journal of Economic History, 8* (1959), 17–32.

Many subjects were touched on in the readings but not elaborated. Foremost among them is the role of Plato as the most influential critic and debunker of both the actual weaknesses and the theory of Athenian democracy at the time of its decline. A group of essays by experts in political science, philosophy, and sociology, collected and edited by Thomas L. Thorson, titled *Plato: Totalitarian or Democrat?* (Englewood Cliffs, N.J., 1963), explore Plato's political writings as the source of either democratic or totalitarian ideology. One of the articles is an extract from a book which is highly recommended as much for its socio-historical method as for its influence on recent scholarship on Plato and democratic thought: Karl Popper, *The Open Society and Its Enemies*, 4th edition, published in two volumes as Harper Torchbook 1101 (New York, 1963). Chapter Ten is especially relevant to the problem of decline. Claude Mossé, in a comprehensive history of the social and political crises in fourth century Athens, *La Fin de la démocratie athénienne* (Paris, 1962) points out that one of the most serious failures was that the remedies for arresting the decline were offered by theoreticians—Plato and Isocrates, for example—who hardly took any account of the disagreeable facts of political life. Their proposals were therefore irrelevant and unworkable.

Though most scholarly opinion agrees that the breakdown came before or, at the latest, by the beginning of the fourth century, Paul Cloché, who has written many valuable studies on Athens, concludes in *La Démocratie athénienne* (Paris, 1955) that democracy was a going concern through most of the fourth century until Athens, like the rest of Greece, was forcibly subjected to Macedonian rule; freedom was, in other words, assassinated.

The intellectual and spiritual failings of the Greeks themselves are sometimes held responsible for, or indicative of, their failure to maintain democracy. Humanism and rationalism have been considered both the foundations for democracy and the causes for its decline. Arnold Toynbee, in his book on *Hellenism* (New York, 1959) advances the theory that the humanism (or "man-worship," as he defines the term) practiced by the Greeks led them to worship the state itself—which led them into a political *cul-de-sac*. As a counterweight to this interpretation of humanism and its consequences, Moses Hadas, *Humanism: The Greek Ideal and Its Survival* (New York, 1960), stresses the positive aspects of humanism and a quite different understanding of the definition of the term and its influence. Henry Bamford Parkes believes that the Athenian debacle "provided a convincing demonstration of the inadequacy of rationalism alone as a guide for human life." The chapters devoted to Greece in his book, *Gods and Men: The Origins of Western Civilization* (New York, 1959), should be read in detail for his analysis of Greek rationalism. This spirit of rationalism, according to Eric R. Dodds, *The Greeks and the Irrational* (Berkeley, Calif., 1951), almost—but not quite—moved into a full-blown Age of Reason, "rode to the jump and refused it," primarily because the Greeks lacked understanding of the irrational in their natures, and failed to cope effectively with what Dodds terms the "return of irrationality." The different intellectual attitudes in Athens, too often irreconcilable, are revealed through an exceedingly interesting study of *Sophocles and Pericles* by Victor Ehrenberg (Oxford, 1954)

Many works might be cited which recognize the failure but stress or defend what was successful in Athenian democracy. There is room here to mention only a few: Walter A. Agard, *What Democracy Meant to the Greeks* (Chapel Hill, North Carolina, 1942); A. H. M. Jones, "The Athenian Democracy and Its Critics," in *Athenian Democracy* (Oxford, 1957); the chapter by T. R. Glover in *Democracy in the Ancient World* (Cambridge, England, 1927) entitled "Periclean Athens"; and Max Cary, "Athenian Democracy," *History*, n.s., *12* (1927), 206–217.